EUTHANASIA

Contemporary Issues

Series Editors: Robert M. Baird
Stuart E. Rosenbaum

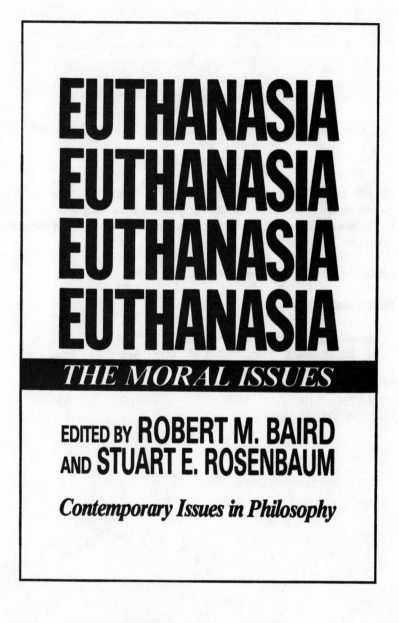

EUTHANASIA
EUTHANASIA
EUTHANASIA
EUTHANASIA

THE MORAL ISSUES

EDITED BY **ROBERT M. BAIRD**
AND **STUART E. ROSENBAUM**

Contemporary Issues in Philosophy

PROMETHEUS BOOKS
BUFFALO, NEW YORK

Published 1989 by Prometheus Books
700 East Amherst Street, Buffalo, New York 14215

Library of Congress Cataloging-in-Publication Data

Euthanasia: The moral issues

    (Contemporary issues in philosophy)
    1. Euthanasia. I. Baird, Robert M., 1937–
II. Rosenbaum, Stuart E. III. Series. [DNLM: 1. Ethics,
Medical. 2. Euthanasia. W 50 E887]
R726.E794   1989   179′.7   89-24042
ISBN 0-87975-555-5 (pbk.)

Contents

6   Contents

Introduction

Stewart Alsop, the respected political columnist, was diagnosed as having leukemia in July, 1971. In sharing the ensuing struggle with his readers, Alsop described the experience of Jack, a hospital roommate.

The third night that I roomed with Jack in our tiny double room in the solid-tumor ward of the cancer clinic of the National Institutes of Health in Bethesda, Maryland, a terrible thought occurred to me.

Jack had a melanoma in his belly, a malignant solid tumor that the doctors guessed was about the size of a softball. The cancer had started a few months before with a small tumor in his left shoulder, and there had been several operations since. The doctors planned to remove the softball-sized tumor, but they knew Jack would soon die. The cancer had metastasized—it had spread beyond control.

Jack was good-looking, about 28, and brave. He was in constant pain, and his doctor had prescribed an intravenous shot of a synthetic opiate—a pain-killer, or analgesic—every four hours. [Jack's] wife spent many of the daylight hours with him, and she would sit or lie on his bed and pat him all over, as one pats a child, only more methodically, and this seemed to help control the pain. But at night, when his pretty wife had left (wives cannot stay overnight at the NIH Clinic) and darkness fell, the pain would attack without pity.

At the prescribed hour, a nurse would give Jack a shot of the synthetic analgesic, and this would control the pain for perhaps two hours or a bit more. Then he would begin to moan, or whimper, very low, as though he didn't want to wake me. Then he would begin to howl, like a dog.

When this happened, either he or I would ring for a nurse, and ask for a pain-killer. She would give him some codeine or the like by mouth, but it never did any real good—it affected him no more than half an aspirin might affect a man who had just broken his arm.

7

Always the nurse would explain as encouragingly as she could that there was not long to go before the next intravenous shot—"only about 50 more minutes now." And always poor Jack's whimpers and howls would become more loud and frequent until at last the blessed relief came.

The third night of this routine, the terrible thought occurred to me. "If Jack were a dog," I thought, "what would be done with him?" The answer was obvious: the pound, and chloroform. No human being with a spark of pity could let a living thing suffer so, to no good end.[1]

Consider a second situation.

On February 24, the son of Mr. and Mrs. Robert H. T. Houle died following court-ordered emergency surgery at Maine Medical Center. The child was born February 9, horribly deformed. His entire left side was malformed; he had no left eye, was practically without a left ear, had a deformed left hand; some of his vertebrae were not fused. Furthermore, he was affected with a tracheal esophageal fistula and could not be fed by mouth. Air leaked into his stomach instead of going to the lungs, and fluid from the stomach pushed up into the lungs. As Dr. Andre Hellegers . . . noted, "It takes little imagination to think [that] there were further internal deformities. . . ."

As the days passed, the condition of the child deteriorated. Pneumonia set in. His reflexes became impaired and because of poor circulation, severe brain damage was suspected. The tracheal esophageal fistula, the immediate threat to his survival, can be corrected with relative ease by surgery. But in view of the associated complications and deformatives, the parents refused their consent to surgery on "Baby Boy Houle." Several doctors in the Main Medical Center felt differently and took the case to court. Maine Superior Court Judge David G. Roberts ordered the surgery to be performed. He ruled: "At the moment of live birth there does exist a human being entitled to the fullest protection of the law. The most basic right enjoyed by every human being is a right to life itself."[2]

Finally, consider a decision scenario generated by Ronald Munson in his work on medical ethics.

Mr. Jeffry Box was eighty-one years old when he was brought to Doctor's Hospital. His right side was paralyzed, he spoke in a garbled way, and he had trouble understanding even the simplest matters. His only known relative was a sister four years younger, and she lived half a continent away. When the hospital social worker called to tell her about her brother's condition, she was quite uninterested. "I haven't seen him in fifteen years," she said. "I thought he might already be dead. Just do whatever you think best for him. I'm too old to worry about him."

Neurological tests and X-ray studies showed Mr. Box was suffering from a brain hemorrhage caused by a ruptured blood vessel.

"Can you fix it?" asked Dr. Hollins. She was the resident responsible for Mr. Box's primary care. The man she addressed was Dr. Carl Oceana, the staff's only neurosurgeon.

"Sure," said Dr. Oceana. "I can repair the vessel and clean out the mess. But it won't do much good, you know."

"You mean he'll still be paralyzed?"

"That's right. And he'll still be mentally incoherent. After the operation he'll have to be put in a nursing home or some other chronic-care place, because he won't be able to see to his own needs."

"And, if you don't operate?" Dr. Hollins asked.

Dr. Oceana shrugged. "He'll be dead by tomorrow. Maybe sooner, depending on how long it takes for the pressure in his skull to build up."

"What would you do?"

"I know what I would want done to me if I were the patient," said Dr. Oceana. "I'd want people to keep their knives out of my head and let me die a nice, peaceful death."

"But we don't know what he would want," Dr. Hollins said. "He's never been our patient before, and the social worker hasn't been able to find any friends who might tell us what he'd want done."

"Let's just put ourselves in his place," said Dr. Oceana. "Let's do unto others what we would want done unto us."

"That means letting Mr. Box die."

"Exactly"[3]

These cases illustrate several reasons for considering euthanasia: the situation of intense pain, the birth of a radically deformed child, and the deterioration that sometimes accompanies aging. The term "euthanasia" is derived from two Greek words (*eu* and *thanatos*) meaning good or easy death. Euthanasia is often called mercy killing because the motivation is to act humanely toward one who is suffering. In cases such as those described above, should death be permitted or   a way of humanely helping the per   ?

The purpose of this book is to pose the moral dilemmas of euthanasia and to provide a collection of essays that present clearly the alternative views. By analyzing the arguments of these essays, readers should be able to reach at least tentative conclusions, and perhaps become better equipped to make difficult decisions of their own concerning these matters.

Crucial in controversial discussions are distinctions that enable the conversation to proceed in a clear way. Concerning euthanasia, several distinctions are helpful.

Because law and morality are so intertwined (laws, for example, often develop out of moral concerns) the distinction between the two is often ignored. But they are different: something moral may not be legal; something legal may not be moral. A law is a rule of conduct prescribed by properly constituted governing authority and enforced by sanctions. Whether or not an action is moral, by contrast, depends upon whether it can be supported by reasons within the framework of a set of moral assumptions, which themselves must be subject to critical appraisal. The collected essays in this volume are concerned primarily with the *moral* permissibility of euthanasia. The legal issue, however, is never far in the background—for two reasons. Most people consider the legality of an act to have a bearing on its morality. Moreover, if a sufficient number of people became persuaded of the moral acceptability of euthanasia, then laws might change, making it legal. Indeed, that is the hope of several writers represented in this volume.

A second important distinction is that between active and passive euthanasia, between overtly killing and "letting die." In active euthanasia the overt killing of the patient by the physician (or some assistant) normally involves "the injection of a lethal dose of a drug (usually a short-acting barbiturate, followed by a paralyzing agent). . . ."[4] This form of active euthanasia is distinct from physician-assisted suicide, where the final act is performed by the patient. Letting die involves omitting the steps necessary to prolong life, such as failing to resuscitate a patient in heart failure, withholding penicillin from an elderly person with pneumonia, or ceasing chemotherapy for a cancer victim. If a physician enters a hospital room and turns off the machines that sustain life, that physician is doing something active, but turning off machines that sustain life is normally thought to be a form of passive euthanasia. The key question is whether the death is directly the result of human intervention (active euthanasia), or the result of natural causes that are permitted to run their course (passive euthanasia).

This distinction is contained in "The Report on the Physician and the Dying Patient" presented by the Judicial Council of the American Medical Association and accepted by the association at its Clinical Convention in December, 1973. The relevant section reads:

> The intentional termination of the life of one human being by another—mercy killing—is contrary to that for which the medical profession stands and is contrary to the policy of the American Medical Association.
>
> The cessation of the employment of extraordinary means to prolong the life of the body when there is irrefutable evidence that biological death is imminent is the decision of the patient and/or his immediate family. The advice and judgment of the physician should be freely available to the patient and/or his immediate family.[5]

The first paragraph of this statement unequivocally opposes active euthanasia; the second permits passive euthanasia. The moral significance of this distinction between active and passive euthanasia is the subject of the written debate, included in this volume, between James Rachels and Thomas Sullivan.

Consider also the distinction between voluntary and involuntary euthanasia. Voluntary euthanasia involves explicit consent by the patient; involuntary euthanasia involves a decision for death by a person or persons other than the patient. Killing or letting die a comatose patient would be an instance of involuntary euthanasia, unless the patient had previously given directions concerning what was to be done in such circumstances. Killing or letting die a newborn with severe birth defects would, of necessity, constitute involuntary euthanasia.

If we take the last two sets of distinctions, four logical possibilities emerge: active voluntary euthanasia, active involuntary euthanasia, passive voluntary euthanasia, and passive involuntary euthanasia.

As the following essays reveal, the two forms of passive euthanasia are widely practiced, and, as we have seen, condoned by the AMA under certain circumstances. Active euthanasia, particularly active voluntary euthanasia, is the form of euthanasia most widely discussed today. While active euthanasia is illegal in all fifty states, increasingly it is defended on moral grounds both by physicians and ethicists, many of whom argue for its legalization. This moral defense of euthanasia has elicited intense opposition. This volume seeks to present a balanced account of the debate.

The opening essay recounts the response of Dax Cowart, a burn victim, to his rescue from death. His attitude will surprise many. This is followed by the anonymous acknowledgment that appeared in a 1988 issue of the *Journal of the American Medical Association,* an acknowledgment by a physician that he had killed a young cancer patient, Debbie, for reasons of mercy. Two brief responses to the "Debbie" case are also included. Because the "Karen Quinlan" case is such an important part of recent euthanasia debate, we have included C. Everett Koop's account of the facts of this nationally publicized case. These opening essays focusing on actual cases are followed by the Rachels-Sullivan exchange referred to above.

After this spirited debate, there follows a series of essays that, in effect, debate the pros and cons of euthanasia. Articles by Koop, Gay-Williams, Coleman, and Shewmon basically oppose it, while material by Fletcher, Young, Admiraal, and Engelhardt support euthanasia under certain circumstances.

The volume concludes with three group statements. The first is a report opposing euthanasia, written by a British Medical Association working party, a report approved by the council of the BMA. The second is a statement in support of euthanasia signed by twenty prominent individuals from the medical, scientific, philosophical, and religious communities. The final article is a provocative piece by twelve physicians appearing in a recent issue of the *New England Journal of Medicine.* It focuses on the question of physician-assisted suicide. Its conclusions may surprise many.

Because of medical, technical, and nutritional advances that prolong life, euthanasia is an issue that will demand an increasing share of society's attention. The editors hope that this volume will contribute to an informed response to the complexity of the euthanasia question.

NOTES

1. Stewart Alsop, "The Right to Die with Dignity," *Good Housekeeping* (August 1974): 69 and 130. This story was first brought to the editors' attention by James Rachels use of it in *The End of Life: Euthanasia and Morality* (Oxford: Oxford University Press, 1986), p. 153.

2. Richard A. McCormick, "To Save or Let Die: The Dilemma of Modern Medicine," *Journal of the American Medical Association* 229 (July 8, 1974): 172. Reprinted in Mappes and Zembaty, *Biomedical Ethics* (New York: McGraw-Hill Book Company, 1981), pp. 379-380.

3. Ronald Munson, *Intervention and Reflection: Basic Issues in Medical Ethics,* Second Edition (Belmont, Calif.: Wadsworth Publishing Company, 1983), p. 181.

4. Sidney H. Wanzer, et. al., "The Physician's Responsibility Toward Hopelessly Ill Patients," *The New England Journal of Medicine* 320 (March 30, 1989): 848. (See chapter 19 of this volume.)

5. *The Journal of the American Medical Association* 227, no. 7 (February 18, 1974): 728.

1

Sentenced to Life

Christine Wicker

It's been sixteen years since the explosion.

He has a law degree now and a new wife who loves him, a swimming pool, four acres of land, and a big stucco house that looks like the Alamo.

But Dax Cowart has never changed his mind. They should have let him die.

No matter that he isn't selling pencils on the street like he said he would be. No matter that he no longer feels any pain from the burns themselves. He's rehabilitated, well-adjusted, financially secure, and "acceptably happy." No matter.

"If you had to do something as deeply painful as skinning someone alive or boiling them in oil in order to keep them alive, would you think it was worth it?" he asks.

"To say my life now justifies the treatment forced on me is to say that the end justifies the means." Something he will never say.

Newspapers call Dax Cowart "The Man Who Was Sentenced to Life," "The Man Who Lives to Defend the Right to Die."

Now forty-one, he uses his life to affirm the right of every sane adult to choose death. He should have refused to pay the medical bills and probably should have sued the doctors who used his mother's

From the *Dallas Morning News* Sunday (April 23, 1989): 1F & 4F. Reprinted by permission of the publisher.

consent to override his wishes, he says. "Probably the reason I didn't is, it would have been very difficult to (sue) and still live in the same house with my mother."

His refusal to admit the superior wisdom of the experts who saved him continues to bedevil and polarize legal and medical professionals. The documentary of his ordeal, *Dax's Case,* was a runner-up in the 1985 American Film Festival. A book of essays on his treatment has just been compiled by Southern Methodist University professor of religious studies Lonnie D. Kliever. It's called *Dax's Case: Essays in Medical Ethics and Human Meaning.*

His voice is heard in the book only through the interpretations of others. But even so, his will resounds. Just as it did in the moments after the explosion.

Dax and his father, Ray, were looking at a piece of land a few miles out of town. Unaware that a nearby pipeline was leaking propane gas, they parked in a low area. When they tried to start the car, a pool of propane ignited, killing Ray and severely burning Dax.

Dax ran through three walls of fire, collapsing about a mile and a half down the road. When a neighboring farmer approached, Dax almost immediately pleaded for a gun, asking "Can't you see I'm a dead man?"

For fourteen months, nurses dipped him almost every day into a tank of Clorox solution and scrubbed his burned skin. It took several people to hold down his atrophied, eighty-five-pound body during the tankings. Then they took him back to bed, where he screamed until, exhausted, he passed out.

All the while, he begged, "Please let me die."

Both hands were amputated, leaving just enough thumb for him to grasp a fork or the handle of a coffee cup. He must use his tongue to dial the phone.

The skin that wasn't burned was sliced for grafts. The only undamaged skin left is on the bottoms of his feet. When he really wants to feel something, he uses his toes.

His ears were damaged. His eyes became infected and had to be removed. In a way, his blindness has been a perverse blessing. It keeps him from seeing how people respond to his face.

But medical and legal professionals say Dax's life is functional, worth preserving. And it is true that he has made it so. "I'm acceptably happy," he says. "Under the circumstances. But of course, my life is much different."

The ramrod straight posture that he had even as a child makes him seem taller than his five feet, nine inches. And when he lounges in a chair, leans on a wall, throws his arm casually over the sofa back to turn toward someone, the athlete's ease of body is still present.

"He was a hunk," says Georgia Moss, the secretary in his law office. "He still is. At least to me, and (his wife) Randy, and everyone who knows him."

He walks into the living room behind his wife and places his nub of a hand on her shoulder. He's smiling, looking right at you with artificial eyes so beautifully blue, so life-like, that you must remind yourself over and over that he is blind.

Dax's nostrils, his lips, his eyelids, all burned off in the accident, have been remolded and patched back onto his face. The scars and skin graphs are a multicolored quilt of ribbed and twisted, stretched and puffed, patched-together bits of skin.

They would make a mask of his face if his personality weren't so strong. But somehow you sense it. And, leaving him, you remember his smile.

When listening to a question, he holds himself absolutely still, sometimes leaning forward to turn his sightless eyes onto the speaker's face with a look of total attention, as though the speaker's voice were his only connection with the world. Because, of course, it is.

His voice, twanging with that flat East Texas accent, is rich and vibrant and full of humor, as though it's never had reason to mourn.

Dax tried to kill himself several times after he was released from the hospital. He tried slashing his wrists, taking sleeping pills. During the year that he lived with his mother, he once slipped out of the house in the night and made his way to a road. When the police found him, he was crouched, listening for gravel trucks, trying to time their passage so that he could know when to throw himself in front of one.

But that despair has largely been relieved, he says. He complains only of frustration.

"He was a party boy," his mother, Ada, says. "And he still is."

It seems an odd statement. But he's so determinedly normal that many people act that way around him—as though nothing is the least bit different about Dax. When driving somewhere with him, people regularly ask his advice about which route to take. Georgia is constantly chiding his best friend and sometime co-counsel Daryll Bennett for ambling off and expecting Dax to follow.

"Daryll will leave him standing all by himself in a room. And then he'll say, 'Well, I forgot.' "

Whenever he and Georgia walk along the street, Dax has her tell him who's coming toward them so that he can greet them as they approach.

A QUESTION OF RIGHTS

Self-pity isn't his style. Neither is rage. "I'm not really bitter about the treatments," he says. "No one had ulterior motives."

Georgia says she's hardly ever seen him depressed, never truly angry. His wife calls him "the nicest, gentlest, most considerate man I know." He is the one who will crawl across the floor after a long day to search for the dog's toy. When a tree was cut down in their yard, it was Dax who lamented that a squirrel has lost its home.

His adamant insistence on the right to die isn't a tantrum or a matter of pride, as some like to believe, he says. It's a matter of rights. As a conscious, sane adult, he should have been able to decide his own fate. "I was completely astonished that, in this country, I could be forced to undergo treatment," he says.

His mother signed the consent papers. She refused to help him find a lawyer to seek a restraining order against the hospital.

Now sixty-five, she still remembers the acrid smell of bleach in the hall outside the immersion tank. She still grieves over her failure to demand more pain medication for him. But, like her son, she has never recanted.

One reason she couldn't let him die was her fear that his unsaved soul would go to hell. He had rejected his parents' Church of Christ teachings long before the accident.

"The way I thought about it was that what he was going through was just a sample of what eternal damnation would be," she says.

She's still praying for his conversion today. And he's still relying on his own indomitable will.

Dax and his mother agree that his anger probably saved him.

His doctor accused Dax of trying to manipulate the staff by

asking them to let him die—a request he knew they could not honor. Another doctor recounts having challenged Dax by saying, "If you're half the man I think you are, if you're what I've been led to believe—the kind of person you were before you were burned—then don't ask us to let you die, because in a sense that means we're killing you."

Dax had been a rodeo champion and an Air Force pilot who flew to Vietnam, a man who liked to drive his convertible Alfa Romeo fast, a skier who favored the steepest hills.

"I've been a competitor as long as I can remember," he says. He played sports despite a slipped disc. He made co-captain of his high school team despite his size. "I always figured that I could overcome whatever physical limitations I had."

Now just a walk across a parking lot can exhaust his damaged legs. Randy, who's a nurse, says that the trauma he's been through seems to have aged his body prematurely.

"It's hard being so dependent," he says, "taking four, five, ten times longer to do anything. I miss being able to pick up the car keys and go like I always had."

LOVING CARE

At a dinner party with friends, Randy positions Dax's fork over each part of the meal so he knows where to reach. She mentions her constant search for movies he saw before the explosion, tells how she has to smuggle him into women's public restrooms. Such grim reminders of his limitations would dampen the conversation if she and Dax were not so matter-of-fact and funny.

When Randy brings up the restroom, Dax jokes about being hidden in a stall one day when he had to say something to Randy. When the woman in the stall next to them heard his voice, "all I heard was the flush, and she was out of there," Dax says.

Dax and Randy are good company. But not many Henderson people visit them. "I think seeing Dax reminds people of how fragile life is. They're reminded that it could happen to them," Randy says.

As grim as it's been, his life hasn't turned out as badly as Dax thought it would. For one thing, he feared that he would never have a relationship with a woman again.

But Randy is his second wife since the explosion, and she wanted to marry him before they ever met.

She was teaching combat medics at the University of Utah 1 1/2 years ago when she showed a film about Dax. A student asked what had happened to him. Although she was certain that he was dead, Randy promised to find out.

She found him in Henderson, and they talked on the phone for two hours. And they talked every day thereafter for two months.

Randy, forty-five, left a boyfriend, a good job, and two grown children. For two days, she begged Dax to marry her. "He gives me more emotionally than anyone ever has," she says. "He would give me anything he could."

Dax told Randy that life with him would be harder than she imagined, and it has been, she says. She worries about money more than she ever did before. The physical work of caring for him and the house and grounds keeps her constantly busy.

Dax hates to be alone. "I can't blame him," Randy says. "If you shut your eyes and plugged your ears and couldn't touch, you'd go crazy if you were alone."

They listen to music together and go to restaurants. She often reads to him. One weekend, they were both so excited about a book that they read almost all night, falling asleep for only a few hours and then beginning to read again as soon as they awakened.

He has trouble sleeping and often has nightmares. Some nights, he dreams that people are all around, stabbing him.

In the end, as much as he compensates, vulnerability is Dax's most constant companion, perhaps the only one certain to draw nearer with time. What he fears most now, he says, is "old age and the infirmity it brings."

Randy understands his fear. "If it were to get worse—if he were paralyzed, lost his hearing or was in great pain—if he asked me to, I would kill him. Of course I would. It's already so bad, I can't see making him endure more.

"And I know that if the same thing were to happen to me, he would kill me. If he could."

The medical world that thwarted his desire to die has gone on about its business. The million-dollar resources available to keep him alive aren't available to help him live the life he's left with.

"If they're going to override a patient's wishes, then they ought to be there to help him override the deficiencies that he's left with," Dax says.

Thanks to an out-of-court settlement with the gas company, plus Randy's salary, they have enough to live on for the rest of their lives. But finding meaningful work is another problem.

There had been talk, when Dax was in law school, of his practicing with a local firm. But when Dax finished school, the firm didn't have room for another lawyer. The lawyers in the firm have helped him by referring some clients and giving advice. So have other lawyers. But the cases Dax has been getting are low-dollar and high-research, not the kind to keep a practice afloat.

TIME TO MOVE

The phone rings at all hours with callers wanting free legal advice, Randy says. "He always gives it to them. And then they go hire somebody else."

"I can't make it as a lawyer in Henderson," he says. "If I'd forseen what's happened in the last two years, I probably would have looked in another direction for a career."

Dax is winding the practice down, and the Cowarts plan to move to Galveston, where he hopes to teach bioethics at the medical school. He's a good teacher and one of the founding members of Henderson's Toastmasters club.

Ada and Dax aren't close anymore. They rarely visit. Their old disagreements, about life and death and God, are deep chasms between them.

Everyone seems to have learned a lesson from what happened to Dax, Ada says. "Everyone's learned something but him. Of course, he has learned that he can go out and survive."

Dax knows that she has his best interests at heart. But he wouldn't agree with her analysis. Not totally, anyway. "It's possible to live a happier life than I ever thought," he says. "I've conceded that for a long time now."

But the real lesson he's learned is that anyone can lose control of his own life in an instant. "People forget about the pain, and they say 'That's in the past and everything's hunky-dory.' But it's not, because if I was injured again, or bedfast, I'd have to go through it again. And so would anyone else."

2

It's Over, Debbie

Anonymous

The call came in the middle of the night. As a gynecology resident rotating through a large, private hospital, I had come to detest telephone calls, because invariably I would be up for several hours and would not feel good the next day. However, duty called, so I answered the phone. A nurse informed me that a patient was having difficulty getting rest, could I please see her. She was on 3 North. That was the gynecologic-oncology unit, not my usual duty station. As I trudged along, bumping sleepily against walls and corners and not believing I was up again, I tried to imagine what I might find at the end of my walk. Maybe an elderly woman with an anxiety reaction, or perhaps something particularly horrible.

I grabbed the chart from the nurses station on my way to the patient's room, and the nurse gave me some hurried details: a twenty-year-old girl named Debbie was dying of ovarian cancer. She was having unrelenting vomiting apparently as the result of an alcohol drip administered for sedation. Hmmm, I thought. Very sad. As I approached the room I could hear loud, labored breathing. I entered and saw an emaciated, dark-haired woman who appeared much older than twenty. She was receiving nasal oxygen, had an IV, and was

From the *Journal of the American Medical Association,* edited by Roxanne K. Young 259, no. 2 (January 8, 1988): 272. Copyright 1988, American Medical Association.

sitting in bed suffering from what was obviously severe air hunger. The chart noted her weight at eighty pounds. A second woman, also dark-haired but of middle age, stood at her right, holding her hand. Both looked up as I entered. The room seemed filled with the patient's desperate effort to survive. Her eyes were hollow, and she had suprasternal and intercostal retractions with her rapid inspirations. She had not eaten or slept in two days. She had not responded to chemotherapy and was being given supportive care only. It was a gallows scene, a cruel mockery of her youth and unfulfilled potential. Her only words to me were, "Let's get this over with."

I retreated with my thoughts to the nurses station. The patient was tired and needed rest. I could not give her health, but I could give her rest. I asked the nurse to draw 20 mg. of morphine sulfate into a syringe. Enough, I thought, to do the job. I took the syringe into the room and told the two women I was going to give Debbie something that would let her rest and to say goodbye. Debbie looked at the syringe, then laid her head on the pillow with her eyes open, watching what was left of the world. I injected the morphine intra-venously and watched to see if my calculations would be correct. Within seconds her breathing slowed to a normal rate, her eyes closed, and her features softened as she seemed restful at last. The older woman stroked the hair of the now-sleeping patient. I waited for the inevitable next effect of depressing the respiratory drive. With clocklike certainty, within four minutes the breathing rate slowed even more, then became irregular, then ceased. The dark-haired woman stood erect and seemed relieved.

It's over, Debbie.

3

Doctors Must Not Kill

Willard Gaylin, Leon R. Kass, Edmund D. Pellegrino, and Mark Siegler

In the middle of the night, a sleepy gynecology resident is called to attend a young woman, dying of cancer, whom he has never seen before. Horrified by her severe distress, and proceeding alone without consultation with anyone, he gives her a lethal injection of morphine, clearly intending the death that promptly ensues. The resident submits a first-person account of his killing to the *Journal of the American Medical Association*. Without any editorial comment, *JAMA* publishes the account, withholding the author's name at his request. What in the world is going on?

Before the sophisticated obscure our vision with clouds of arguments and subtle qualifications, we must fix our gaze on the brute facts.

First, on his own admission, the resident appears to have committed a felony: premeditated murder. Direct intentional homicide is a felony in all American jurisdictions, for which the plea of merciful motive is no excuse. That the homicide was clearly intentional is confirmed by the resident's act of unrepentant publication.

Second, law aside, the physician behaved altogether in a scan-

From the *Journal of the American Medical Association* 259, no. 14 (April 8, 1988): 2139-2140. Copyright 1988, American Medical Association.

dalously unprofessional and unethical manner. He did not know the patient: he had never seen her before, he did not study her chart, he did not converse with her or her family. He never spoke to *her* physician. He took as an unambiguous command her only words to him, "Let's get this over with": he did not bother finding out what precisely she meant or whether she meant it wholeheartedly. He did not consider alternative ways of bringing her relief or comfort; instead of comfort, he gave her death. This is no humane and thoughtful physician succumbing with fear and trembling to the pressures and well-considered wishes of a patient well known to him, for whom there was truly no other recourse. This is, by his own account, an impulsive yet cold technician, arrogantly masquerading as a knight of compassion and humanity. (Indeed, so cavalier is the report and so cold-blooded the behavior, it strains our credulity to think that the story is true.)

Third, law and professional manner both aside, the resident violated one of the first and most hallowed canons of the medical ethic: doctors must not kill. Generations of physicians and commentators on medical ethics have underscored and held fast to the distinction between ceasing useless treatments (or allowing to die) and active, willful taking of life; at least since the Oath of Hippocrates, Western medicine has regarded the killing of patients, even on request, as a profound violation of the deepest meaning of the medical vocation. As recently as 1986, the Judicial Council of the American Medical Association, in an opinion regarding treatment of dying patients, affirmed the principle that a physician "should not intentionally cause death." Neither legal tolerance nor the best bedside manner can ever make medical killing medically ethical.

The conduct of the physician is inexcusable. But the conduct of the editor of *JAMA* is incomprehensible. By publishing this report, he knowingly publicizes a felony and shields the felon. He deliberately publicizes the grossest medical malfeasance and shields the malefactor from professional scrutiny and judgment, presumably allowing him to continue his practices without possibility of rebuke and remonstrance, not even from the physician whose private patient he privately dispatched. Why? For what possible purpose central to *JAMA's* professional mission?

According to newspaper reports, the editor of *JAMA* published the article "to promote discussion" of a timely and controversial topic.

But is this a responsible way for the prestigious voice of our venerable profession to address the subject of medical killing? Is it morally responsible to promulgate challenges to our most fundamental moral principles without editorial rebuke or comment, "for the sake of discussion"? Decent folk do not deliberately stir discussion of outrageous practices, like slavery, incest, or killing those in our care.

What is to be done? Regarding the case at hand, the proper course is clear. *JAMA* should voluntarily turn all the information it has regarding the case over to the legal authorities in the pertinent jurisdictions. The physician's name should also be reported to his hospital directors and to his state and county medical societies for their scrutiny and action. The Council on Ethical and Judicial Affairs of the American Medical Association should examine the case, as well as the decision to publish it. Justice requires nothing less.

But much more is at stake than punishing an offender. The very soul of medicine is on trial. For this is not one of those peripheral issues about which pluralism and relativism can be tolerated, about which a value-free stand on the substance can be hedged around with procedural safeguards to ensure informed consent or "sound decision making." Nor is this an issue, like advertising, fee-splitting, or cooperation with chiropractors, that touches medicine only as a trade. This issue touches medicine at its very moral center; if this moral center collapses, if physicians become killers or are even merely licensed to kill, the profession—and, therewith, each physician—will never again be worthy of trust and respect as healer and comforter and protector of life in all its frailty. For if medicine's power over life may be used equally to heal or to kill, the doctor is no more a moral professional but rather a morally neutered technician.

These are perilous times for our profession. The Hemlock Society and others are in the courts and legislatures trying to legalize killing by physicians at patient request. Such a proposal is almost certainly going to be on the ballot in California next November.* High costs of care for the old and incurable already tempt some physicians to regard as "dispensable" some patients who never express the wish to die. In the Netherlands, where the barriers to physician killing are gone, there are now many well-documented cases of such cryptic and "uninvited" killing by doctors.[1]

---

*The initiative to place this item on the ballot failed to secure sufficient support and thus did not appear as these authors anticipated.—Eds.

Now is not the time for promoting neutral discussion. Rather, now is the time for the medical profession to rally in defense of its fundamental moral principles, to repudiate any and all acts of direct and intentional killing by physicians and their agents. We call on the profession and its leadership to obtain the best advice, regarding both theory and practice, about how to defend the profession's moral center and to resist growing pressures both from without and from within. We call on fellow physicians to say that we will not deliberately kill. We must also say to each of our fellow physicians that we will not tolerate killing of patients and that we shall take disciplinary action against doctors who kill. And we must say to the broader community that if it insists on tolerating or legalizing active euthanasia, it will have to find nonphysicians to do its killing.

NOTE

1. R. Fenigsen, *Euthanasia: Een Weldaad (Charitable Euthanasia).* Deventer, the Netherlands, Van Loghum Slaterus, 1987.

4

Debbie's Dying
Mercy Killing and the Good Death

Kenneth L. Vaux

Most of the condemnatory response to "It's Over, Debbie"[1] has rightly claimed that what (apparently) transpired that night was unconscionable. One does not stumble angrily into the night and decide profound matters of life and death for another human being. This strange narrative does not tell us whether Debbie wanted simply to be relieved of pain or released from intolerable suffering; whether the family consented or what the nurses or chaplains on call advised; or whether the attending or primary physician, if one existed, authorized the action. The whole process, from beginning to end, was morally unacceptable.

A deeper question, however, lies behind the widespread interest in this one reprehensible action—the question that troubles us all. As I lie dying, will I be offered humane care, will I be done in too soon by some expediency, or will I be subjected to terminal torture?

Euthanasia does not refer to Nazi-like elimination of the sick, old, or unproductive, and, because it lacks any account of patient consent, "It's Over, Debbie" is in no way an accurate representation of any form of euthanasia. Traditionally, euthanasia means the search

From the *Journal of the American Medical Association* 259, no. 14 (April 8, 1988): 2141. Copyright 1988, American Medical Association.

for a good death, an easier death for one who is dying, a death released in some measure from intractable suffering. It assumes and requires the patient's unequivocal request and the consent of the family. Our best medical and religious traditions accept euthanasia when it assists the person who is imminently dying toward a less devastating and more peaceful demise. Passive euthanasia *often,* double-effect euthanasia *sometimes,* and active euthanasia *rarely* have become established as a morally acceptable continuum of action in our ethical tradition.

One reading of this ambiguous and melodramatic diary suggests that Debbie's case may be one of *double-effect* euthanasia: the patient died as a result of medication given in an attempt to relieve pain and with the knowledge that it would hasten death. Morphine is not normally a poison but an analgesic drug, and 20 mg. is scarcely a murderous dose. The physician could not possibly have known with the brash confidence that his narrative displays that his injection would kill. More likely, he sought to provide relief and rest to this dying young woman, knowing that it would speed her death. In the pursuit of a legitimate, indeed obligatory, purpose of relieving suffering, he shortened the remaining hours of her life. If this is a true rendition of Debbie's case, it represents an instance of morally acceptable double-effect euthanasia (or what is technically called *agathanasia,* a better death). The side effect is unfortunate, indeed grievous, but it is not unethical.

The President's Commission report on *Decisions to Forego Life-Sustaining Treatment*[2] and many cancer care texts hold that it is permissible to use analgesic treatment for end-stage cancer pain and respiratory distress even if it hastens death. As the President's Commission report states,

> No death is more agonizing for the aware patient . . . than one from respiratory insufficiency. Untreated, the patient will struggle for air until exhausted, when carbon dioxide narcosis and progressive hypoxia finally bring death fairly quickly. With the consent of the family morphine may be given. . . . If the patient is already quite exhausted, the slowed respirations will induce hypercapnia, which will perpetuate the sedation and the patient will die in the ensuing sleep.

What about intentional mercy killing—active and direct euthanasia? Is such action ever medically or ethically acceptable? Even if it is proscribed, can it be excused from legal prosecution or professional censure? Down through the ages, when the patient and physician have established a clear understanding and the physician's desire has been to relieve the patient's incurable pain, most cases of mercy killing have been excused by virtue of the spirit rather than the letter of the law. In all noble jurisprudence and even more in the ethics of caring for the dying, absolutist principles must always be chastened by mercy.

I argue that while positive euthanasia must be proscribed in principle, in exceptional cases it may be abided in deed. There has always been a place, albeit carefully restricted to a limited range of cases, for voluntary euthanasia. From classical times throughout the Christian centuries and into modern secular society, this allowance has always existed alongside the dominant ethic of prolonging and sustaining life. There are numerous cases today in the medical and legal case files in which active euthanasia has been reluctantly allowed and the physicians involved have not been prosecuted. In his classic of medical ethics, *The Patient as Person,*[3] Paul Ramsey, Ph.D., a spokesman for traditional ethics, makes unrelenting cancer pain an exception to the dominant ethic of "doing nothing to place the dying more quickly beyond our love and care." Here, "one can hardly be held morally blameworthy if in these instances dying is directly accomplished or hastened."

Philosophical ethics aside, the most moving evidence I have witnessed for this viewpoint in my twenty-five years as a consultant in medical ethics is the testimony of highly ethical and humane physicians. Although impeded by law and custom from giving a lethal dose to their patient, these physicians would, in fact, do so even at risk of prosecution for their wife or father or child if the patient was suffering in such end-of-life agony as Debbie.

That physicians and nurses would request euthanasia of their colleagues or would assist their own loved ones to have a more merciful death but would deny it to their patients says something about the moral nature of the act. Such loving acts illustrate a kind of "exception" ethic that has a place in the tradition of alleviating suffering.

The position of "exception-case" active euthanasia is grounded in classical clinical wisdom. In the Hippocratic tradition, the physician was discouraged from therapeutically or technologically invading the atrium of death. Attempts to cure had to yield to attempts to comfort.

An ethical principle that later transformed Western medicine held that the living ought never to be treated as if they were dying, nor the dying as if they were living. To know the difference entailed discerning the *signum Hippocraticum* (the signs of mortality).

In recent years the qualities that morally distinguished the living from the dying have been blurred. With our life-prolonging techniques and medications, we have transformed death; we have taken it out of the acute, natural, and noninterventional mode and made it more into a chronic, contrived, and manipulated phenomenon. Deaths as inevitable as Debbie's have been protracted by a range of interventions, including chemotherapy (disrupting the cellular-pathogenic process), analgesia (altering the release of natural body endorphins and narcotics), the administration of intravenous fluids and nutrients, and hospitalization itself. Logically and emotionally, we cannot intervene at one phase and then be inactive at another, more painful phase. We cannot modify nature and then plead that nature must be allowed to run its unhindered course.

Medicine is a pastoral art, especially when a good physician, like a good shepherd, accompanies a patient "into the valley of the shadow." Here the dying one must indeed "fear no evil," either the evil of weary dispatch or of principled withdrawal.

Where does this leave us? The outrage of Debbie's case reminds us that we must never abandon the cardinal purpose of medical care—to save and sustain life and never intentionally to harm or kill. The other lesson of this case is that we must not destroy the virtue of that commitment by using medical art to prolong dying and puritanically refuse to relieve suffering. This distortion is very possible today, when technological prowess is joined to low rates of bed occupancy and economic distress in hospitals and when our society tends to deny the inevitability of death. If biomedical acts of life extension become acts of death prolongation, we may force some patients to outlive their deaths, and we may ultimately repudiate the primary life-saving and merciful ethic itself.

NOTES

1. "It's Over, Debbie," A Piece of My Mind, *Journal of the American Medical Association (JAMA)* 259 (1988): 272. (See this volume chapter 2.)

2. "Supportive Care for Dying Patients," in *Decisions to Forego Life-Sustaining Treatment,* President's Commission for the Study of Ethical Problems in Medicine and Biomedical and Behavioral Research (1983): 294-295.

3. P. Ramsey, *The Patient as Person* (New Haven, Conn.: Yale University Press, 1983), p. 163.

5

The Case of Karen Quinlan

C. Everett Koop

The name Karen Quinlan became identified in the autumn of 1975 in the minds of all who are concerned about matters of life and death with the extraordinary possibility of the termination of life becoming a legal matter. In piecing the story together, *Time* Magazine wrote it this way.[1] Karen Ann Quinlan had been born of unknown parents in Pennsylvania and was adopted by Mr. and Mrs. Joseph Quinlan when she was four weeks old. *Time* said that the Quinlans considered her to be a friendly, outgoing girl, a fine skier and swimmer, and one who sang in their church. Karen's friends in high school, from which she graduated in 1972, described her as quiet but popular with the boys. Her employer, who discharged her because of a company cutback in August of 1974, remembered her as a good, hard worker.

Apparently in the last few months of her active life Karen, after losing her job, moved out of her parents' home and into employment and friendships unlike her previous lifestyle. ". . . Somewhere along the line, she began experimenting with drugs. Several friends described her as an occasional marijuana user and frequent pill popper who took 'uppers' and 'downers' to suit her moods."[2]

Time concluded that drugs were probably responsible for Karen's

From *The Right to Live; The Right to Die,* by C. Everett Koop. Wheaton, Ill.: Tyndale House Publishers, Inc., 1976, pp. 102-111. All rights reserved. Reprinted by permission of the publisher.

current condition. On April 14th, apparently depressed, she not only took some tranquilizers but then went to a bar to celebrate her friend's birthday. After drinking gin and tonic, she began to "nod out." Friends took Karen home and put her to bed, where she passed out. It was realized that she was more than drunk. Attempts were made to revive her with mouth-to-mouth resuscitation; an ambulance was called. She never regained consciousness.

It is important to recognize . . . that Karen was then presented as an emergency situation to the local community hospital where, without much knowledge of what had happened before, the immediate resuscitative measures, including the use of a respirator, were probably begun. To have taken time in gaining a history that would have revealed all that is known months later, would have forfeited the one opportunity Karen's doctors had to restore her to active life. It is also worth mentioning that many people presented to the emergency room of a hospital with the same signs and symptoms are treated exactly as Karen was and recover, most of those recovering having their full faculties.

Time reports that Karen's parents kept hoping that she would recover and were looking for a miracle. Mr. Quinlan's own parish priest feared that Mr. Quinlan was losing touch with reality in this regard.

Karen had been in a coma since the early morning of April 15, her breathing maintained by a mechanical device called a respirator. By all accounts reported in *Time,* she had shriveled into something scarcely human: she weighed only sixty pounds, was unable to move a muscle, to speak, or to think. This was the picture presented to the world through the news media when in September of 1975 the doctors caring for Karen refused Mr. Quinlan's request to pull the electric plug from the respirator, thereby terminating her life. Mr. Quinlan then sued for his child's right to die, putting it in his own religious terms: "In my own mind, I had already resolved this spiritually through my prayers, and I had placed Karen's body and soul into the gentle, loving hands of the Lord. . . . It was resolved that we would turn the machine off."[3]

There were several facts that were not immediately made known in the media and which have never been clarified in the minds of many who have criticized the eventual decision of Superior Court Judge Robert Muir, Jr., when he finally decided on November 10th that the doctors could not disconnect the life-sustaining respirator from Karen Ann Quinlan's body and allow her to die.*

The first of these facts was that Karen was alive. The fact that it was reported that she could not move a muscle was not completely true, because she did respond to pain and cried when pinched. Although her electroencephalographic tracing (electrical brain waves) was not normal, it did show electrical activity, which in this gray netherland between life and death has been interpreted over and over again by medical experts to indicate that the brain is still alive, even though it may not appear to think or function. Although many of the medical experts appearing as expert witnesses at the trial agreed that Karen was like a child without a brain, nevertheless they insisted that the machine could not be turned off. The consensus was that Karen met none of the medically accepted criteria for determining death. In other words, in spite of her situation she had not had "brain death," which is the legal definition of death in the eight states that have statutes concerning this matter. (New Jersey, where this trial took place, is not one of them.)†

The second fact was that although many medical decisions are not to *start* the use of an extraordinary life-support mechanism such as a respirator, once the decision *is* made to start such (I have already indicated that there was really no alternative to this decision at the time Karen was presented to her emergency room physicians), then with a living organism who has not exhibited brain death, to turn off the life-support mechanism is to deliberately produce death. This act is, in the minds of those interested in intricacies of both law and medicine, homicide.

Third, the whole conduct of medical care these days is governed to a large extent by the shadow of malpractice suits hanging over the medical profession. There are lawyers who say there has never been a relationship between a physician and a patient in which they cannot find a cause for a medical malpractice suit. Whereas in days gone by, medical malpractice centered around not practicing medicine

---

*Muir's decision was unanimously reversed by the Supreme Court of New Jersey on March 31, 1976.—Eds.

†By 1988, twenty-five states had adopted the Uniform Determination of Death Act that superseded the 1980 Uniform Brain Death Act. The Uniform Determination of Death Act provides for determination of death based upon irreversible loss of all brain functions. New Jersey is still not among the twenty-five states that acknowledge brain death.—Eds.

in conformity with the standards of the community, now medical malpractice suits are instituted because the result is less than perfect or less than the patient or his family expected in a given encounter with disease or surgery. Obviously, the specter of malpractice litigation hung over the doctors who were requested to disconnect the respirator from the body of Karen Quinlan.

During the trial a number of things were discussed in the press, not only as news reports but in analyses by people both competent and incompetent to make such analyses. It was clear that whereas it can be argued with conviction that there is a right to live guaranteed by our Constitution (but apparently not applicable to the unborn child), there is no "right to die" under that same Constitution. In fact, many legal actions work in the opposite direction. Members of the Jehovah's Witnesses sect have been legally shown not to have the right to refuse a blood transfusion on religious grounds nor to withhold such from a minor who has not reached the age of consent. It is also legal practice for the courts to appoint guardians for children in order that they will be given adequate medical treatment that parents, for multiple reasons, are unwilling to provide.

Franklin Zimring, professor of law at the University of Chicago, put the matter succinctly in reference to the proper place for decisions of this kind to be made: "Some decisions are beyond the law's competence to make with any rigor or confidence in being right."[4]

There was legal eloquence with theological overtones from such competent and respected jurists as Ralph Porzio, who is not new to these concerns, having written a book in recent years concerning the multitudinous problems of life and death which arise around the medical transplantation of organs from one person to the other. He asked these questions:

"Dare we defy the undisputed premise, the granite foundation of this case, that Karen Ann Quinlan is legally and medically alive?"

"Dare we defy nature's immutable command to survive?"

"Dare we defy the divine command, 'Thou shalt not kill'?"[5]

Many analysts tried to condense into one newspaper column a synthesis of religious and moral teaching of the three major religions in the United States: Judaism, Catholicism, and Protestantism. All of these fell short of anything like reaching the mark because there is no monolithic theological or religious teaching about this matter in any of these religions. What may be the personal, sincere conviction of the Quinlan's parish priest might not be what the Vatican thinks on the same subject. Although Orthodox Judaism has as high a regard for the sanctity of human life based upon the Old Testament Scriptures as can be found in our culture, the younger generation practicing Reform Judaism does not hold to this same high opinion nor does it base its decisions on Scripture. In the Protestant religion, not only are there innumerable denominational differences, but within the denominations both liberal and conservative differences. If one were to ask a situational ethicist such as Joseph Fletcher, he might tell you that death control is the same as birth control. On the other hand an ethicist such as Paul Ramsey, who bases his decisions on the Bible, which he considers to be the Word of God, says it this way: "Attention paid to God's dominion means man has only stewardship over life." And, "Proper stewardship can involve deciding how to live the last days of (one's) life."[6]

I interrupt this train of thought to recall once again to the reader's mind that there is a distinct difference in the mind of the practicing physician who deals with these matters day in and day out between not starting a life support extraordinary technique because he feels it would produce a "Karen Quinlan," and, once having made the decision to start it, terminating it—which is a deliberate act, ending the life of a patient, interpreted by many as homicide.

In mid-November, in a forty-four page ruling, Judge Robert Muir, Jr., discounted "the compassion, sympathy he felt toward the Quinlan family" and went on to say that both "judicial conscience and morality" told him that Karen's fate was being handled properly by "the treating physician." Under common law, he said, (in spite of) "the fact that the victim is on the threshold of death," no "humanitarian motives" can justify taking life. He dismissed "semantics" by which he referred to questions about whether disconnecting Karen's body from the respirator would be an act of commission or omission. Either would result in the taking of her life, which the law says is homicide. Judge Muir clearly stated that "there is no constitutional right to die that can be asserted by a parent for his incompetent adult child."[7]

It is worthwhile to consider the arguments that were presented by Karen Quinlan's lawyers because they are the arguments that come into the mind of any reader of the press in circumstances that are so reported.

1. "Medical science holds no hope for Miss Quinlan's recovery."

   In fact, doctors at the trial had indicated that there is always a possibility of recovery although not as a human being with cerebral function. The judge concluded that if such were possible, "what level or plateau she will reach is unknown."

2. "Miss Quinlan would want the respirator turned off."

   Mr. Quinlan had stated that his daughter had made statements like this before her concomitant taking of alcohol and drugs [which] somehow put her into the situation which produced her discerebrate condition, causing coma. The judge noted that even if these had been the wishes of Miss Quinlan when she was well and happy it was not when she was "under solemn and sobering fact that death was a distinct choice."

3. "Doctors have no legal obligation to keep Miss Quinlan alive."

   The judge believed that such a duty exists when the physician believes that she should be kept alive. Judge Muir very properly stated that a patient placed in the care of a doctor expects that the doctor "will do all within his human power to favor life against death."

4. "The wishes of the parents of an incompetent patient should be paramount in a doctor's life-or-death decision."

   The judge took a contrary point of view because "there is always the dilemma of whether it is the conscious being's belief or the conscious being's welfare that governs the parental motivation."

5. "The constitutional right of privacy should allow parents or guardians to make the decision that an incompetent child's life should no longer be prolonged."

   Judge Muir believed that all previous right-to-privacy cases concerned rights to maintain a lifestyle, not rights to end life altogether.

6. "Freedom of religion should allow Miss Quinlan, a Roman Catholic, to die."

Judge Muir felt that the previous interpretations of the right to exercise religious beliefs, as enunciated by the United States Supreme Court, dealt with life on earth, not life hereafter.

7. "The beauty and meaning of Karen's life was over and she should be allowed to die."

Judge Muir indicated, again rightly so, that nowadays the use of a respirator as an emergency measure in a patient in Karen Quinlan's condition (as it was the night she was presented to the emergency room of the local hospital) was really an ordinary, rather than extraordinary, step in medical practice. He said, "Continuation of medical treatment, in whatever form, where its goal is sustenance of life, is not something degrading, arbitrarily inflicted, unacceptable to contemporary society, or unnecessary."[8]

In the days that followed Judge Muir's decision, editorial comment in general was in favor of the jurists' point of view and those who knew best about the laws of the land recognized that the laws we now have currently forbid anyone from giving permission to any other person to pull the plug on a life-sustaining machine. The judge knows when he is asked to give this permission that it is productive of homicide. In that sense, this entire trial was a futile exercise. Somebody should have been able to say at the start that no judge could rightly tell someone else to commit a homicide. After the emotional furor associated with the trial had quieted down, most agreed that the right of Karen to die was not a matter for the courts. This was all well and good, but it opened speculation in another area that could be just as bad.

Most editorial comment, after agreeing that Karen's problem was not a matter for the courts, attributed this to archaic or obsolete laws—and this is wrong. If it were not even called a homicide, just to pose an argument, it is impossible for a jurist or, even worse, a jury to make a decision, even when they have all of the pertinent facts such as are available in the case of Karen Quinlan. How then can legislators establish laws on the right to die when Karen Quinlan's problem is only one of literally hundreds that exist, all with different reasons and motivations, and with their attendant emotional overlay?[9]

If well-meaning legislators, pressured by public opinion rising out of the emotional concern around the Karen Quinlan case or others like it, should push several of the United States to formulate laws concerning the right to die, Pandora's box will have been opened to expose a situation that really has no solution. We are dealing with medicine, with technology, and with law. Basic to the relationship between physician and patient is the expectation that life is worthy to be lived, that physicians will act on behalf of their patients toward this end, and that if acts of omission or commission lead to an earlier demise of a patient than might ordinarily have been expected, *these decisions have to remain within the bounds of the expected, compassionate, understanding relationship between the patient and his doctor and the patient's family and the patient's doctor.* The number of examples of this decision making is legion. It is unthinkable that the law could direct this decision making on the part of the physician, because to do so would undermine the fundamental principles in all of the great field of health care.

In reviewing a case history like that of Karen Quinlan the decisions are difficult enough and fraught with sufficient danger to give anyone pause even if he confines his attention to concern for the patient and consideration for the patient's family. But since human beings are what they are, if it were possible for the law, in its cold impersonal way, to direct decision making on the part of a physician concerning life and death, other motives would very quickly enter the picture. Whereas it can be argued that all the motives in the Karen Quinlan case are pure, the opportunity for base, evil, calculating, conniving motives is wide open if the decision-directed death could be demanded of a physician by way of the law. Without our knowing it, it is the Judeo-Christian concept of the sanctity of human life, even respected by an areligious people, that makes it possible for us to live day by day in the relative security of the obviously imperfect, poorly defined parameters of decision making concerning death and dying in medicine. To remove the decision making from the person primarily involved, namely the physician, and to place it in the hands of the law, would remove that security and expose each of us, first, to improper and inappropriate decisions at the time of death. Further, with the erosion of the morality which would necessarily take place, those decisions would be moved closer and closer to vibrant life instead of being confined to the area of waning life.[10]

NOTES

1. *Time* Magazine (November 3, 1975):52.

2. Ibid.

3. Ibid.

4. Ibid., p. 58.

5. *Sunday Times Advertiser,* Trenton, N.J. (November 2, 1975).

6. Paul Ramsey, "The Indignity of Death with Dignity," *Hastings Center Study* (May 1974).

7. *Time* Magazine (November 24, 1975):70.

8. Much of the seven questions have been taken from the excellent analysis of Aaron Epstein, a staff writer of the *Philadelphia Inquirer,* reported in that newspaper November 11, 1975.

9. Editorial, *The Philadelphia Inquirer* (November 12, 1975). William A. Reusher, Op-Ed page. *The Philadelphia Inquirer* (November 23, 1975).

10. At the time of this writing, a question has been raised concerning Karen Quinlan's condition when she was presented to the emergency room of her community hospital April 15. She had an egg-size bump on her head as well as a series of bruises on her body that had been received shortly before admission (*Time* [December 29, 1975]).

6

Active and Passive Euthanasia

James Rachels

The distinction between active and passive euthanasia is thought to be crucial for medical ethics. The idea is that it is permissible, at least in some cases, to withhold treatment and allow a patient to die, but it is never permissible to take any direct action designed to kill the patient. This doctrine seems to be accepted by most doctors, and it is endorsed in a statement adopted by the House of Delegates of the American Medical Association on December 4, 1973:

> The intentional termination of the life of one human being by another—mercy killing—is contrary to that for which the medical profession stands and is contrary to the policy of the American Medical Association.
>
> The cessation of the employment of extraordinary means to prolong the life of the body when there is irrefutable evidence that biological death is imminent is the decision of the patient and/or his immediate family. The advice and judgment of the physician should be freely available to the patient and/or his immediate family.

However, a strong case can be made against this doctrine. In what follows I will set out some of the relevant arguments, and urge doctors to reconsider their views on this matter.

From *The New England Journal of Medicine* 292, no. 2 (January 9, 1975): 78-80. Copyright 1975 Massachusetts Medical Society.

To begin with a familiar type of situation, a patient who is dying of incurable cancer of the throat is in terrible pain, which can no longer be satisfactorily alleviated. He is certain to die within a few days, even if present treatment is continued, but he does not want to go on living for those days since the pain is unbearable. So he asks the doctor for an end to it, and his family joins in the request.

Suppose the doctor agrees to withhold treatment, as the conventional doctrine says he may. The justification for his doing so is that the patient is in terrible agony, and since he is going to die anyway, it would be wrong to prolong his suffering needlessly. But now notice this. If one simply withholds the treatment, it may take the patient longer to die, and so he may suffer more than he would if more direct action were taken and a lethal injection given. This fact provides strong reason for thinking that, once the initial decision not to prolong his agony has been made, active euthanasia is actually preferable to passive euthanasia, rather than the reverse. To say otherwise is to endorse the option that leads to more suffering rather than less, and is contrary to the humanitarian impulse that prompts the decision not to prolong his life in the first place.

Part of my point is that the process of being "allowed to die" can be relatively slow and painful, whereas being given a lethal injection is relatively quick and painless. Let me give a different sort of example. In the United States about one in 600 babies is born with Down's syndrome. Most of these babies are otherwise healthy—that is, with only the usual pediatric care, they will proceeed to an otherwise normal infancy. Some, however, are born with congenital defects such as intestinal obstructions that require operations if they are to live. Sometimes, the parents and the doctor will decide not to operate, and let the infant die. Anthony Shaw describes what happens then:

> . . . When surgery is denied [the doctor] must try to keep the infant from suffering while natural forces sap the baby's life away. As a surgeon whose natural inclination is to use the scalpel to fight off death, standing by and watching a salvageable baby die is the most emotionally exhausting experience I know. It is easy at a conference, in a theoretical discussion, to decide that such infants should be allowed to die. It is altogether different to stand by in the nursery and watch as dehydration and infection wither a tiny being over hours and days. This is a terrible ordeal for me and the hospital staff—much more so than for the parents who never set foot in the nursery.[1]

I can understand why some people are opposed to all euthanasia, and insist that such infants must be allowed to live. I think I can also understand why other people favor destroying these babies quickly and painlessly. But why should anyone favor letting "dehydration and infection wither a tiny being over hours and days"? The doctrine that says that a baby may be allowed to dehydrate and wither, but may not be given an injection that would end its life without suffering, seems so patently cruel as to require no further refutation. The strong language is not intended to offend, but only to put the point in the clearest possible way.

My second argument is that the conventional doctrine leads to decisions concerning life and death made on irrelevant grounds.

Consider again the case of the infants with Down's syndrome who need operations for congenital defects unrelated to the syndrome to live. Sometimes, there is no operation, and the baby dies, but when there is no such defect, the baby lives on. Now, an operation such as that to remove an intestinal obstruction is not prohibitively difficult. The reason why such operations are not performed in these cases is, clearly, that the child has Down's syndrome and the parents and doctor judge that because of that fact it is better for the child to die.

But notice that this situation is absurd, no matter what view one takes of the lives and potentials of such babies. If the life of such an infant is worth preserving, what does it matter if it needs a simple operation? Or, if one thinks it better that such a baby should not live on, what difference does it make that it happens to have an unobstructed intestinal tract? In either case, the matter of life and death is being decided on irrelevant grounds. It is the Down's syndrome, and not the intestines, that is the issue. The matter should be decided, if at all, on that basis, and not be allowed to depend on the essentially irrelevant question of whether the intestinal tract is blocked.

What makes this situation possible, of course, is the idea that when there is an intestinal blockage, one can "let the baby die," but when there is no such defect there is nothing that can be done, for one must not "kill" it. The fact that this idea leads to such results as deciding life or death on irrelevant grounds is another good reason why the doctrine should be rejected.

One reason why so many people think that there is an important moral difference between active and passive euthanasia is that they think killing someone is morally worse than letting someone die. But is it? Is killing, in itself, worse than letting die? To investigate this issue, two cases may be considered that are exactly alike except that one involves killing whereas the other involves letting someone die. Then, it can be asked whether this difference makes any difference to the moral assessments. It is important that the cases be exactly alike, except for this one difference, since otherwise one cannot be confident that it is this difference and not some other that accounts for any variation in the assessments of the two cases. So, let us consider this pair of cases:

In the first, Smith stands to gain a large inheritance if anything should happen to his six-year-old cousin. One evening while the child is taking his bath, Smith sneaks into the bathroom and drowns the child, and then arranges things so that it will look like an accident.

In the second, Jones also stands to gain if anything should happen to his six-year-old cousin. Like Smith, Jones sneaks in planning to drown the child in his bath. However, just as he enters the bathroom Jones sees the child slip and hit his head, and fall face down in the water. Jones is delighted; he stands by, ready to push the child's head back under if it is necessary, but it is not necessary. With only a little thrashing about, the child drowns all by himself, "accidentally," as Jones watches and does nothing.

Now Smith killed the child, whereas Jones "merely" let the child die. That is the only difference between them. Did either man behave better, from a moral point of view? If the difference between killing and letting die were in itself a morally important matter, one should say that Jones's behavior was less reprehensible than Smith's. But does one really want to say that? I think not. In the first place, both men acted from the same motive, personal gain, and both had exactly the same end in view when they acted. It may be inferred from Smith's conduct that he is a bad man, although that judgment may be withdrawn or modified if certain further facts are learned about him—for example, that he is mentally deranged. But would not the very same thing be inferred about Jones from his conduct? And would not the same further considerations also be relevant to any modification of this judgment? Moreover, suppose Jones pleaded, in his own defense, "After all, I didn't do anything except just stand there and watch the child drown. I didn't kill him; I only let him die." Again, if letting die were in itself less bad than killing, this defense should have at least some weight. But it does not. Such a "defense" can only be regarded as a grotesque perversion of moral reasoning. Morally speaking, it is no defense at all.

Now, it may be pointed out, quite properly, that the cases of euthanasia with which doctors are concerned are not like this at all. They do not involve personal gain or the destruction of normal, healthy children. Doctors are concerned only with cases in which the patient's life is of no further use to him, or in which the patient's life has become or will soon become a terrible burden. However, the point is the same in these cases: The bare difference between killing and letting die does not, in itself, make a moral difference. If a doctor lets a patient die, for humane reasons, he is in the same moral position as if he had given the patient a lethal injection for humane reasons. If his decision was wrong—if, for example, the patient's illness was in fact curable—the decision would be equally regrettable no matter which method was used to carry it out. And if the doctor's decision was the right one, the method used is not in itself important.

The AMA policy statement isolates the crucial issue very well; the crucial issue is "the intentional termination of the life of one human being by another." But after identifying this issue, and forbidding "mercy killing," the statement goes on to deny that the cessation of treatment is the intentional termination of a life. This is where the mistake comes in, for what is the cessation of treatment, in these circumstances, if it is not "the intentional termination of the life of one human being by another"? Of course it is exactly that, and if it were not, there would be no point to it.

Many people will find this judgment hard to accept. One reason, I think, is that it is very easy to conflate the question of whether killing is, in itself, worse than letting die, with the very different question of whether most actual cases of killing are more reprehensible than most actual cases of letting die. Most actual cases of killing are clearly terrible (think, for example, of all the murders reported in the newspapers), and one hears of such cases every day. On the other hand, one hardly ever hears of a case of letting die, except for the actions of doctors who are motivated by humanitarian reasons. So one learns to think of killing in a much worse light than of letting die. But this does not mean that there is something about killing that makes it in itself worse than letting die, for it is not the bare difference between killing and letting die that makes the difference in these cases. Rather, the other factors—the murderer's motive of personal gain, for example, contrasted with the doctor's humanitarian motivation—account for different reactions to the different cases.

I have argued that killing is not in itself any worse than letting die; if my contention is right, it follows that active euthanasia is not any worse than passive euthanasia. What arguments can be given on the other side? The most common, I believe, is the following:

"The important difference between active and passive euthanasia is that, in passive euthanasia, the doctor does not do anything to bring about the patient's death. The doctor does nothing, and the patient dies of whatever ills already afflict him. In active euthanasia, however, the doctor does something to bring about the patient's death: he kills him. The doctor who gives the patient with cancer a lethal injection has himself caused his patient's death; whereas if he merely ceases treatment, the cancer is the cause of the death."

A number of points need to be made here. The first is that it is not exactly correct to say that in passive euthanasia the doctor does nothing, for he does do one thing that is very important: he lets the patient die. "Letting someone die" is certainly different, in some respects, from other types of action—mainly in that it is a kind of action that one may perform by way of not performing certain other actions. For example, one may let a patient die by way of not giving medication, just as one may insult someone by way of not shaking his hand. But for any purpose of moral assessment, it is a type of action nonetheless. The decision to let a patient die is subject to moral appraisal in the same way that a decision to kill him would be subject to moral appraisal: it may be assessed as wise or unwise, compassionate or sadistic, right or wrong. If a doctor deliberately let a patient die who was suffering from a routinely curable illness, the doctor would certainly be to blame for what he had done, just as he would be to blame if he had needlessly killed the patient. Charges against him would then be appropriate. If so, it would be no defense at all for him to insist that he didn't "do anything." He would have done something very serious indeed, for he let his patient die.

Fixing the cause of death may be very important from a legal point of view, for it may determine whether criminal charges are brought against the doctor. But I do not think that this notion can be used to show a moral difference between active and passive euthanasia. The reason why it is considered bad to be the cause of someone's death is that death is regarded as a great evil—and so it is. However, if it has been decided that euthanasia—even passive euthanasia—is desirable in a given case, it has also been decided that in this instance death is no greater an evil than the patient's continued existence. And if this is true, the usual reason for not wanting to be the cause of someone's death simply does not apply.

Finally, doctors may think that all of this is only of academic interest—the sort of thing that philosophers may worry about but that has no practical bearing on their own work. After all, doctors must be concerned about the legal consequences of what they do, and active euthanasia is clearly forbidden by the law. But even so, doctors should also be concerned with the fact that the law is forcing upon them a moral doctrine that may well be indefensible, and has a considerable effect on their practices. Of course, most doctors are not now in the position of being coerced in this matter, for they do not regard themselves as merely going along with what the law requires. Rather, in statements such as the AMA policy statement that I have quoted, they are endorsing this doctrine as a central point of medical ethics. In that statement, active euthanasia is condemned not merely as illegal but as "contrary to that for which the medical profession stands," whereas passive euthanasia is approved. However, the preceding considerations suggest that there is really no moral difference between the two, considered in themselves (there may be important moral differences in some cases in their consequences, but, as I pointed out, these differences may make active euthanasia, and not passive euthanasia, the morally preferable option). So, whereas doctors may have to discriminate between active and passive euthanasia to satisfy the law, they should not do any more than that. In particular, they should not give the distinction any added authority and weight by writing it into official statements of medical ethics.

NOTE

1. A. Shaw, "Doctor, Do We Have a Choice?" *The New York Times Magazine* (January 30, 1972): 54.

7

Active and Passive Euthanasia: An Impertinent Distinction?

Thomas D. Sullivan

Because of recent advances in medical technology, it is today possible to save or prolong the lives of many persons who in an earlier era would have quickly perished. Unhappily, however, it often is impossible to do so without committing the patient and his or her family to a future filled with sorrows. Modern methods of neurosurgery can successfully close the opening at the base of the spine of a baby born with severe myelomeningocoele, but do nothing to relieve the paralysis that afflicts it from the waist down or to remedy the patient's incontinence of stool and urine. Antibiotics and skin grafts can spare the life of a victim of severe and massive burns, but fail to eliminate the immobilizing contractions of arms and legs, the extreme pain, and the hideous disfigurement of the face. It is not surprising, therefore, that physicians and moralists in increasing number recommend that assistance should not be given to such patients, and that some have even begun to advocate the deliberate hastening of death by medical means, provided informed consent has been given by the appropriate parties.

Reprinted with permission from the Summer 1977 issue of the *Human Life Review*. Copyright 1977 by The Human Life Foundation, 150 East 35 Street, New York, New York 10016 ($15.00 per year).

The latter recommendation consciously and directly conflicts with what might be called the "traditional" view of the physician's role. The traditional view, as articulated, for example, by the House of Delegates of the American Medical Association in 1973 declared:

> The intentional termination of the life of one human being by another—mercy killing—is contrary to that for which the medical profession stands and is contrary to the policy of the American Medical Association.
>
> The cessation of the employment of extraordinary means to prolong the life of the body when there is irrefutable evidence that biological death is imminent is the decision of the patient and/or his immediate family. The advice and judgment of the physician should be freely available to the patient and/or his immediate family.

Basically this view involves two points: (1) that it is impermissible for the doctor or anyone else to terminate intentionally the life of a patient, but (2) that it is permissible in some cases to cease the employment of "extraordinary means" of preserving life, even though the death of the patient is a foreseeable consequence.

Does this position really make sense? Recent criticism charges that it does not. The heart of the complaint is that the traditional view arbitrarily rules out all cases of intentionally acting to terminate life, but permits what is in fact the moral equivalent, letting patients die. This accusation has been clearly articulated by James Rachels in a widely read article that appeared in a recent issue of the *New England Journal of Medicine,* entitled "Active and Passive Euthanasia."[1] By "active euthanasia" Rachels seems to mean *doing something* to bring about a patient's death, and by "passive euthanasia," not doing anything, i.e., just letting the patient die. Referring to the AMA statement, Rachels sees the traditional position as always forbidding active euthanasia, but permitting passive euthanasia. Yet, he argues, passive euthanasia may be in some cases morally indistinguishable from active euthanasia, and in other cases even worse. To make his point he asks his readers to consider the case of a Down's syndrome baby with an intestinal obstruction that could easily be remedied through routine surgery. Rachels comments:

> I can understand why some people are opposed to all euthanasia and insist that such infants must be allowed to live. I think I can also understand why other people favor destroying these babies quickly

and painlessly. But why should anyone favor letting "dehydration and infection wither a tiny being over hours and days"? The doctrine that says that a baby may be allowed to dehydrate and wither, but may not be given an injection that would end its life without suffering, seems so patently cruel as to require no further refutation.[2]

Rachels's point is that decisions such as the one he describes as "patently cruel" arise out of a misconceived moral distinction between active and passive euthanasia, which in turn rests upon a distinction between killing and letting die that itself has no moral importance.

One reason why so many people think that there is an important difference between active and passive euthanasia is that they think killing someone is morally worse than letting someone die. But is it? . . . To investigate this issue two cases may be considered that are exactly alike except that one involves killing whereas the other involves letting someone die. Then, it can be asked whether this difference makes any difference to the moral assessments. . . .

In the first, Smith stands to gain a large inheritance if anything should happen to his six-year-old cousin. One evening while the child is taking his bath, Smith sneaks into the bathroom and drowns the child, and then arranges things so that it will look like an accident.

In the second, Jones also stands to gain if anything should happen to his six-year-old cousin. Like Smith, Jones sneaks in planning to drown the child in his bath. However, just as he enters the bathroom Jones sees the child slip and hit his head, and fall face down in the water. Jones is delighted; he stands by, ready to push the child's head back under if necessary, but it is not necessary. With only a little thrashing about, the child drowns all by himself, "accidentally," as Jones watches and does nothing.[3]

Rachels observes that Smith killed the child, whereas Jones "merely" let the child die. If there's an important moral distinction between killing and letting die, then, we should say that Jones's behavior from a moral point of view is less reprehensible than Smith's. But while the law might draw some distinctions here, it seems clear that the acts of Jones and Smith are not different in any important way, or, if there is a difference, Jones's action is even worse.

In essence, then, the objection to the position adopted by the AMA of Rachels and those who argue like him is that it endorses a highly questionable moral distinction between killing and letting die, which, if accepted, leads to indefensible medical decisions. Nowhere does Rachels quite come out and say that he favors active euthanasia in some cases, but the implication is clear. Nearly everyone holds that it is sometimes pointless to prolong the process of dying and that in those cases it is morally permissible to let a patient die even though a few hours or days could be salvaged by procedures that would also increase the agonies of the dying. But if it is impossible to defend a general distinction between letting people die and acting to terminate their lives directly, then it would seem that active euthanasia also may be morally permissible.

Now what shall we make of all this? It *is* cruel to stand by and watch a Down's [syndrome] baby die an agonizing death when a simple operation would remove the intestinal obstruction, but to offer the excuse that in failing to operate we didn't *do* anything to bring about death is an example of moral evasiveness comparable to the excuse Jones would offer for his action of "merely" letting his cousin die. Furthermore, it is true that if someone is trying to bring about the death of another human being, then it makes little difference from the moral point of view if his purpose is achieved by action or by malevolent omission, as in the cases of Jones and Smith.

But if we acknowledge this, are we obliged to give up the traditional view expressed by the AMA statement? Of course not. To begin with, we are hardly obliged to assume the Jones-like role Rachels assigns the defender of the traditional view. We have the option of operating on the Down's baby and saving its life. Rachels mentions that possibility only to hurry past it as if that is not what his opposition would do. But, of course, that is precisely the course of action most defenders of the traditional position would choose.

Secondly, while it may be that the reason some rather confused people give for upholding the traditional view is that they think killing someone is always worse than letting them die, nobody who gives the matter much thought puts it that way. Rather they say that killing someone is clearly morally worse than not killing them, and killing them can be done by acting to bring about their death or by refusing ordinary means to keep them alive in order to bring about the same goal.

What I am suggesting is that Rachels's objections leave the position he sets out to criticize untouched. It is worth noting that the jargon of active and passive euthanasia—and it is jargon—does not appear in the resolution. Nor does the resolution state or imply the distinction Rachels attacks, a distinction that puts a moral premium on overt behavior—moving or not moving one's parts—while totally ignoring the intentions of the agent. That no such distinction is being drawn seems clear from the fact that the AMA resolution speaks approvingly of ceasing to use extraordinary means in certain cases, and such withdrawals might easily involve bodily movement, for example unplugging an oxygen machine.

In addition to saddling his opposition with an indefensible distinction it doesn't make, Rachels proceeds to ignore one that it does make—one that is crucial to a just interpretation of the view. Recall the AMA allows the withdrawal of what it calls extraordinary means of preserving life; clearly the contrast here is with ordinary means. Though in its short statement those expressions are not defined, the definition Paul Ramsey refers to as standard in his book, *The Patient as Person,* seems to fit.

> Ordinary means of preserving life are all medicines, treatments, and operations, which offer a reasonable hope of benefit for the patient and which can be obtained and used without excessive expense, pain, and other inconveniences.
> Extraordinary means of preserving life are all those medicines, treatments, and operations which cannot be obtained without excessive expense, pain, or other inconvenience, or which, if used, would not offer a reasonable hope of benefit.[4]

Now with this distinction in mind, we can see how the traditional view differs from the position Rachels mistakes for it. The traditional view is that the intentional termination of human life is impermissible, irrespective of whether this goal is brought about by action or inaction. Is the action or refraining *aimed at* producing a death? Is the termination of life *sought, chosen or planned?* Is the intention deadly? If so, the act or omission is wrong.

But we all know it is entirely possible that the unwillingness of a physician to use extraordinary means for preserving life may be prompted not by a determination to bring about death, but by other motives. For example, he may realize that further treatment may offer little hope of reversing the dying process and/or be excruciating, as in the case when a massively necrotic bowel condition in a neonate is out of control. The doctor who does what he can to comfort the infant but does not submit it to further treatment or surgery may foresee that the decision will hasten death, but it certainly doesn't follow from that fact that he intends to bring about its death. It is, after all, entirely possible to foresee that something will come about as a result of one's conduct without intending the consequence or side effect. If I drive downtown, I can foresee that I'll wear out my tires a little, but I don't drive downtown with the intention of wearing out my tires. And if I choose to forego my exercises for a few days, I may think that as a result my physical condition will deteriorate a little, but I don't omit my exercise with a view to running myself down. And if you have to fill a position and select Green, who is better qualified for the post than her rival Brown, you needn't appoint Mrs. Green with the intention of hurting Mr. Brown, though you may foresee that Mr. Brown will feel hurt. And if a country extends its general education programs to its illiterate masses, it is predictable the suicide rate will go up, but even if the public officials are aware of this fact, it doesn't follow that they initiate the program with a view to making the suicide rate go up. In general, then, it is not the case that all foreseeable consequences and side effects of our conduct are necessarily intended. And it is because the physician's withdrawal of extraordinary means can be otherwise motivated than by a desire to bring about the predictable death of the patient that such action cannot categorically be ruled out as wrong.

But the refusal to use ordinary means is an altogether different matter. After all, what is the point of refusing assistance which offers reasonable hope of benefit to the patient without involving excessive pain or other inconvenience? How could it be plausibly maintained that the refusal is not motivated by a desire to bring about the death of the patient? The traditional position, therefore, rules out not only direct actions to bring about death, such as giving a patient a lethal injection, but malevolent omissions as well, such as not providing minimum care for the newborn.

The reason the AMA position sounds so silly when one listens to arguments such as Rachels's is that he slights the distinction between ordinary and extraordinary means and then drums on cases where *ordinary* means are refused. The impression is thereby conveyed that the traditional doctrine sanctions omissions that are morally indistinguishable in a substantive way from direct killings, but then incomprehensibly refuses to permit quick and painless termination of life. If the traditional doctrine would approve of Jones's standing by with a grin on his face while his young cousin drowned in a tub, or letting a Down's baby wither and die when ordinary means are available to preserve its life, it would indeed be difficult to see how anyone could defend it. But so to conceive the traditional doctrine is simply to misunderstand it. It is not a doctrine that rests on some supposed distinction between "active" and "passive euthanasia," whatever those words are supposed to mean, nor on a distinction between moving and not moving our bodies. It is simply a prohibition against intentional killing, which includes both direct actions and malevolent omissions.

To summarize—the traditional position represented by the AMA statement is not incoherent. It acknowledges, or more accurately, insists upon the fact that withholding ordinary means to sustain life may be tantamount to killing. The traditional position can be made to appear incoherent only by imposing upon it a crude idea of killing held by none of its more articulate advocates.

Thus the criticism of Rachels and other reformers, misapprehending its target, leaves the traditional position untouched. That position is simply a prohibition of murder. And it is good to remember, as C. S. Lewis once pointed out:

> No man, perhaps, ever at first described to himself the act he was about to do as Murder, or Adultery, or Fraud, or Treachery. . . . And when he hears it so described by other men he is (in a way) sincerely shocked and surprised. Those others "don't understand." If they knew what it had really been like for him, they would not use those crude "stock" names. With a wink or a titter, or a cloud of muddy emotion, the thing has slipped into his will as something not very extraordinary, something of which, rightly understood in all of his peculiar circumstances, he may even feel proud.[5]

I fully realize that there are times when those who have the noble duty to tend the sick and the dying are deeply moved by the sufferings of their patients, especially of the very young and the very old, and desperately wish they could do more than comfort and companion them. Then, perhaps, it seems that universal moral principles are mere abstractions having little to do with the agony of the dying. But of course we do not see best when our eyes are filled with tears.

NOTES

1. *The New England Journal of Medicine,* 292 (January 9, 1975): 78-80. (Reprinted, this volume, see chapter 6.)

2. Ibid., pp. 78-79. (This volume, p. 47.)

3. Ibid., p. 79. (This volume, pp. 47–48.)

4. Paul Ramsey, *The Patient as Person* (New Haven and London: Yale University Press, 1970), p. 122. Ramsey abbreviates the definition first given by Gerald Kelly, S.J., *Medico-Moral Problems* (St. Louis, Missouri: *The Catholic Hospital Association,* 1958), p. 129.

5. C. S. Lewis, *A Preface to Paradise Lost* (London and New York: Oxford University Press, 1970), p. 126.

8

More Impertinent Distinctions

James Rachels

Many thinkers, including almost all orthodox Catholics, believe that euthanasia is immoral. They oppose killing patients in any circumstances whatever. However, they think it is all right, in some special circumstances, to allow patients to die by withholding treatment. The American Medical Association's policy statement on mercy killing supports this traditional view. In my paper "Active and Passive Euthanasia"[1] I argued, against the traditional view, that there is in fact no moral difference between killing and letting die—if one is permissible, then so is the other.

Professor Sullivan[2] does not dispute my argument; instead he dismisses it as irrelevant. The traditional doctrine, he says, does not appeal to or depend on the distinction between killing and letting die. Therefore, arguments against that distinction "leave the traditional position untouched."

Is my argument really irrelevant? I don't see how it can be. As Sullivan himself points out,

> Nearly everyone holds that it is sometimes pointless to prolong the process of dying and that in those cases it is morally permissible to let a patient die even though a few more hours or days could be salvaged by procedures that would also increase the agonies of the

dying. But if it is impossible to defend a general distinction between letting people die and acting to terminate their lives directly, then it would seem that active euthanasia also may be morally permissible.[3]

But traditionalists like Professor Sullivan hold that active euthanasia—the direct killing of patients—is *not* morally permissible; so, if my argument is sound, their view must be mistaken. I cannot agree, then, that my argument "leaves the traditional position untouched."

However, I shall not press this point. Instead I shall present some further arguments against the traditional position, concentrating on those elements of the position which Professor Sullivan himself thinks most important. According to him, what is important is, first, that we should never *intentionally* terminate the life of a patient, either by action or omission, and second, that we may cease or omit treatment of a patient, knowing that this will result in death, only if the means of treatment involved are *extraordinary.*

INTENTIONAL AND NONINTENTIONAL TERMINATION OF LIFE

We can, of course, distinguish between what a person does and the intention with which he does it. But what is the significance of this distinction for ethics?

> The traditional view [says Sullivan] is that the intentional termination of human life is impermissible irrespective of whether this goal is brought about by action or inaction. Is the action or refraining *aimed at* producing death? Is the termination of life *sought, chosen, or planned?* Is the intention deadly? If so, the act or omission is wrong.[4]

Thus on the traditional view there is a very definite sort of moral relation between act and intention. An act which is otherwise permissible may become impermissible if it is accompanied by a bad intention. The intention makes the act wrong.

There is reason to think that this view of the relation between act and intention is mistaken. Consider the following example. Jack visits his sick and lonely grandmother, and entertains her for the afternoon. He loves her and his only intention is to cheer her up. Jill also visits the grandmother, and provides an afternoon's cheer.

But Jill's concern is that the old lady will soon be making her will; Jill wants to be included among the heirs. Jack also knows that his visit might influence the making of the will, in his favor, but that is no part of his plan. Thus Jack and Jill do the very same thing— they both spend an afternoon cheering up their sick grandmother— and what they do may lead to the same consequences, namely influencing the will. But their intentions are quite different.

Jack's intention was honorable and Jill's was not. Could we say on that account that what Jack did was right, but what Jill did was wrong? No; for Jack and Jill did the very same thing, and if they did the same thing, we cannot say that one acted rightly and the other wrongly.[5] Consistency requires that we assess similar actions similarly. Thus if we are trying to evaluate their *actions,* we must say about one what we say about the other.

However, if we are trying to assess Jack's *character,* or Jill's, things are very different. Even though their actions were similar, Jack seems admirable for what he did, while Jill does not. What Jill did— comforting an elderly sick relative—was a morally good thing, but we would not think well of her for it since she was only scheming after the old lady's money. Jack, on the other hand, did a good thing *and* he did it with an admirable intention. Thus we think well, not only of what Jack did, but of Jack.

The traditional view, as presented by Professor Sullivan, says that the intention with which an act is done is relevant to determining whether the act is right. The example of Jack and Jill suggests that, on the contrary, the intention is not relevant to deciding whether the *act* is right or wrong, but instead it is relevant to assessing the character of the person who does the act, which is very different.

Now let us turn to an example that concerns more important matters of life and death. This example is adapted from one used by Sullivan himself.[6] A massively necrotic bowel condition in a neonate is out of control. Dr. White realizes that further treatment offers little hope of reversing the dying process and will only increase the suffering; so, he does not submit the infant to further treatment— even though he knows that this decision will hasten death. However, Dr. White does not seek, choose, or plan that death, so it is not part of his intention that he baby dies.

Dr. Black is faced with a similar case. A massively necrotic bowel condition in a neonate is out of control. He realizes that further treatment offers little hope of saving the baby and will only increase its suffering. He decides that it is better for the baby to die a bit sooner than to go on suffering pointlessly; so, with the intention of letting the baby die, he ceases treatment.

According to the traditional position, Dr. White's action was acceptable, but Dr. Black acted wrongly. However, this assessment faces the same problem we encountered before. Dr. White and Dr. Black did *the very same thing:* their handling of the cases was identical. Both doctors ceased treatment, knowing that the baby would die sooner, and both did so because they regarded continued treatment as pointless, given the infants' prospects. So how could one's action be acceptable and the other's not? There was, of course, a subtle difference in their *attitudes* toward what they did. Dr. Black said to himself, "I want this baby to die now, rather than later, so that it won't suffer more; so I won't continue the treatment." A defender of the traditional view might choose to condemn Dr. Black for this, and say that his character is defective (although I would not say that); but the traditionalist should not say that Dr. Black's *action* was wrong on that account, at least not if he wants to go on saying that Dr. White's action was right. A pure heart cannot make a wrong act right; neither can an impure heart make a right act wrong. As in the case of Jack and Jill, the intention is relevant, not to determining the rightness of actions, but to assessing the character of the people who act.

There is a general lesson to be learned here. The rightness or wrongness of an act is determined by the reasons for it or against it. Suppose you are trying to decide, in this example, whether treatment should be continued. What are the reasons for and against this course of action? On the one hand, if treatment is ceased the baby will die very soon. On the other hand, the baby will die eventually anyway, even if treatment is continued. It has no chance of growing up. Moreover, if its life is prolonged, its suffering will be prolonged as well, and the medical resources used will be unavailable to others who would have a better chance of a satisfactory cure. In light of all this, you may well decide against continued treatment. But notice that there is no mention here of anybody's intentions. The intention you would have, if you decided to cease treatment, is not one of the things you need to consider. It is not among the reasons either for or against the action. That is why it is irrelevant to determining whether the action is right.

In short, a person's intention is relevant to an assessment of his character. The fact that a person intended so-and-so by his action may be a reason for thinking him a good or a bad person. But the intention is not relevant to determining whether the act itself is morally right. The rightness of the act must be decided on the basis of the objective reasons for or against it. It is permissible to let the baby die, in Sullivan's example, because of the facts about the baby's condition and its prospects—nto because of anything having to do with anyone's intentions. Thus the traditional view is mistaken on this point.

ORDINARY AND EXTRAORDINARY MEANS OF TREATMENT

The American Medical Association policy statement says that life-sustaining treatment may sometimes be stopped if the means of treatment are "extraordinary"; the implication is that "ordinary" means of treatment may not be withheld. The distinction between ordinary and extraordinary treatments is crucial to orthodox Catholic thought in this area, and Professor Sullivan reemphasizes its importance: he says that, while a physician may sometimes rightly refuse to use extraordinary means to prolong life, "the refusal to use ordinary means is an altogether different matter."[7]

However, upon reflection it is clear that it is sometimes permissible to omit even very ordinary sorts of treatments.

> Suppose that a diabetic patient long accustomed to self-administration of insulin falls victim to terminal cancer, or suppose that a terminal cancer patient suddenly develops diabetes. Is he in the first case obliged to continue, and in the second case obliged to begin, insulin treatment and die painfully of cancer, or in either or both cases may the patient choose rather to pass into diabetic coma and an earlier death? . . . What of the conscious patient suffering from painful incurable disease who suddenly gets pneumonia? Or an old man slowly deteriorating who from simply being inactive and recumbent gets pneumonia: Are we to use antibiotics in a likely successful attack upon this disease which from time immemorial has been called "the old man's friend"?[8]

These examples are provided by Paul Ramsey, a leading theological ethicist. Even so conservative a thinker as Ramsey is sympathetic with the idea that, in such cases, life-prolonging treatment is not mandatory: the insulin and the antibiotics need not be used. Yet surely insulin and antibiotics are "ordinary" treatments by today's medical standards. They are common, easily administered, and cheap. There is nothing exotic about them. So it appears that the distinction between ordinary and extraordinary means does not have the significance traditionally attributed to it.

But what of the *definitions* of "ordinary" and "extraordinary" means which Sullivan provides? Quoting Ramsey, he says that

> Ordinary means of preserving life are all medicines, treatments, and operations, which offer a reasonable hope of benefit for the patient and which can be obtained and used without excessive expense, pain, and other inconveniences.
>
> Extraordinary means of preserving life are all those medicines, treatments, and operations which cannot be obtained without excessive expense, pain, or other inconvenience, or which, if used, would not offer a reasonable hope of benefit. [9]

Do these definitions provide us with a useful distinction—one that can be used in determining when a treatment is mandatory and when it is not?

The first thing to notice is the way the word "excessive" functions in these definitions. It is said that a treatment is extraordinary if it cannot be obtained without *excessive* expense or pain. But when is an expense "excessive"? Is a cost of $10,000 excessive? If it would save the life of a young woman and restore her to perfect health, $10,000 does not seem excessive. But if it would only prolong the life of Ramsey's cancer-stricken diabetic a short while, perhaps $10,000 is excessive. The point is not merely that what is excessive changes from case to case. The point is that what is excessive *depends on* whether it would be a good thing for the life in question to be prolonged.

Second, we should notice the use of the word "benefit" in the definitions. It is said that ordinary treatments offer a reasonable hope of *benefit* for the patient; and that treatments are extraordinary if they will not benefit the patient. But how do we tell if a treatment will benefit the patient? Remember that we are talking about life-prolonging treatments; the "benefit," if any, is the continuation of life. Whether continued life is a benefit depends on the details of the particular case. For a person with a painful terminal illness, a temporarily continued life may not be a benefit. For a person in irreversible coma, such as Karen Quinlan, continued biological existence is almost certainly not a benefit. On the other hand, for a person who can be cured and resume a normal life, life-sustaining treatment definitely is a benefit. Again, the point is that in order to decide whether life-sustaining treatment is a benefit we must *first* decide whether it would be a good thing for the life in question to be prolonged.

Therefore, these definitions do not mark out a distinction that can be used to help us decide when treatment may be omitted. We cannot by using the definitions identify which treatments are extraordinary, and then use that information to determine whether the treatment may be omitted. For the definitions require that we must *already* have decided the moral questions of life and death *before* we can answer the question of which treatments are extraordinary!

We are brought, then, to this conclusion about the distinction between ordinary and extraordinary means. If we apply the distinction in a straightforward, commonsense way, the traditional doctrine is false, for it is clear that it is sometimes permissible to omit ordinary treatments. On the other hand, if we define the terms as suggested by Ramsey and Sullivan, the distinction is useless in practical decision making. In either case, the distinction provides no help in formulating an acceptable ethic of letting die.

SUMMARY

The distinction between killing and letting die has no moral importance; on that Professor Sullivan and I agree. He, however, contends that the distinctions between intentional and nonintentional termination of life, and ordinary and extraordinary means, must be at the heart of a correct moral view. I believe that the arguments given above refute this view. Those distinctions are no better than the first one. The traditional view is mistaken.

In my original paper I did not argue in favor of active euthanasia. I merely argued that active and passive euthanasia are equivalent: *if* one is acceptable, so is the other. However, Professor Sullivan correctly inferred that I do endorse active euthanasia: I believe that it is in some instances morally justified, and that it ought to be made legal.[10] This he believes to be pernicious. In his penultimate paragraph he says that the traditional doctrine "is simply a prohibition of murder," and that those of us who think otherwise are confused, teary-eyed sentimentalists. But the traditional doctrine is not that. It is a muddle of indefensible claims, backed by tradition but not by reason.

NOTES

1. James Rachels, "Active and Passive Euthanasia," *The New England Journal of Medicine,* 292 (January 9, 1975): 78-80. (See this volume, chapter 6.)

2. Thomas D. Sullivan, "Active and Passive Euthanasia: An Impertinent Distinction?" *The Human Life Review,* 3 (1977): 40-46. (See this volume, chapter 7.)

3. Ibid., this volume, p. 57.

4. Ibid., this volume, p. 57.

5. It might be objected that they did not "do the same thing," for Jill manipulated and deceived her grandmother, while Jack did not. If their actions are described in this way, then it may seem that "what Jill did" was wrong, while "what Jack did" was not. However, this description of what Jill did incorporates her intention into the description of the act. In the present context we must keep the act and the intention separate, in order to discuss the relation between them. If they *cannot* be held separate, then the traditional view makes no sense.

6. Sullivan, op. cit., this volume, pp. 57-58.

7. Ibid., this volume, p. 58.

8. Paul Ramsey, *The Patient as Person* (New Haven, Conn.: Yale University Press, 1970), pp. 115-116.

9. Sullivan, op. cit., this volume, p. 57.

10. For arguments in support of this position, see J. Rachels, "Euthanasia," in *Matters of Life and Death,* edited by Tom Regan (New York: Random House, 1979).

9

The Right to Die:
The Moral Dilemmas

C. Everett Koop

The term *euthanasia* comes from the Greek and means painless, happy death (*eu*—well, plus *thanatos*—death). Webster's dictionary goes on to define euthanasia as "an easy and painless death, or, an act or method of causing death painlessly so as to end suffering: advocated by some as a way to deal with victims of incurable disease." The Euthanasia Society of America, founded in 1938, defines euthanasia as the "termination of human life by painless means for the purpose of ending severe physical suffering." Gradually the meaning of one word changed from the connotation of easy death to the actual medical deed necessary to make death easy. Finally it reached the connotation of "mercy killing." The idea that abortion is not killing is a brand new idea. However, the fact that euthanasia is not killing has really never existed. The common synonym for euthanasia in both lay and professional vocabularies has been mercy killing. In any discussion of euthanasia an understanding of terminology is essential. The deliberate killing of one human being by another, no matter what the motivation might be, is murder. Some distinction is usually made

From "Euthanasia" in *The Right to Live; The Right to Die,* by C. Everett Koop. Wheaton, Ill.: Tyndale House Publishers, Inc., 1976, pp. 88–117. All rights reserved. Reprinted by permission of the publisher.

between a positive, decisive, death-producing act and the act of permitting death to occur by withholding life-support mechanism or life-extending procedures which in common parlance might be called heroic and in medical terminology might be called "extraordinary means."

The current discussions of the right to die are, in essence, a broad reflection on the moral and ethical problems created by an understanding of the term *euthanasia*. A consideration of the right to die carries with it the implication of the right of *how* to die. Does a patient have the right to expect a painless, comfortable death? Does he have the right to expect that his physician should see that it is so? Does he have the right to expect that the physician might take an active role in his dying process to shorten it for the sake of the patient's comfort or peace of mind? Does the patient have the right to expect the physician to terminate his life if the physician deems it advisable? Could this ever be an active role on the part of the physician or may he assume only a passive role? Is there a difference between an active and a passive role in this regard; is a deed of omission less reprehensible than a deed of commission legally, ethically, or morally? Does the patient have the right to participate in the decision, or better yet, to influence it?

The way one answers any of these questions will depend a good deal upon his view of life. If he is God-oriented in the sense of being either a conservative follower of Judaism or if he is a Christian, and if he indeed believes that the Scriptures are the Word of God and teach that life is precious to God, he will view life as a holy thing, its end not to be decided upon by man. Yet, many physicians who truly believe that the Scriptures are the Word of God and that they give specific admonitions concerning the sanctity of life, will, in the role of physician, act passively in certain circumstances rather than carry out what the laity might call heroic measures to prolong life.

If, on the other hand, the individual's view of life is atheistic, agnostic, or utilitarian, his decisions about participating in the dying process actively or passively are not so much matters of conscience. In between these two views will probably lie the great majority of people who are faced with this kind of decision making, either as a privilege or an obligation. Although they might not wish to carry the label of a situational ethicist, they would in general be making decisions on the basis of the situation. The situation would encompass for them the patient's state of health, his alertness, his understanding of what was happening to him, and his spoken desires on the matter. But all these would be in the light of the physician's understanding of that patient's disease and that patient's ability to withstand it at all, to withstand it comfortably, or to succumb to it quickly or slowly. One can already see that several physicians might have completely different points of view in a given situation depending upon their previous knowledge of the disease entity in question but also tempered by their previous experience in similar situations where they had been proven right or wrong or where their ethical decisions were affected by the morality which grows out of experience and contact with repetitive problems.

Another facet that the situational ethicist must deal with is the situation in respect to the patient's family. In many situations, for example, there comes a time when the patient's consideration is essentially out of the picture. The patient may be unconscious, truly comatose, definitely out of pain, and waiting for an inevitable death which may be days, weeks, months, or in rare situations even years away. There are emotional factors to be considered in reference to the family and there are definitely economic factors. There may be times when these economic factors may have far-reaching implications. The financial undergirding for the education of a child, for example, might disappear while an unconscious grandmother has her financial substance eaten up by medical bills. The motivation on the part of a family to see a rapid demise in a dying grandmother would understandably be varied but one can see the obvious temptation for a change in motivation as the aforementioned hypothetical example drags on and on.

Can the physician who is in the business of prolonging life and relieving the suffering of the sick and injured be asked to reverse his role and shorten life even while ministering to the needs of the suffering? How much credence should he give to the pressures of the family to terminate life? How can he sort out the motivation that leads to the request? How can he balance his obligation to his patient against his compassion and his understanding for the family? If the right to live and the whole question of killing an unborn baby in the womb raises multiple dilemmas, they are as nothing compared to the dilemmas that are inherent in the question of the right to die. . . .

EXTENSION OF HUMAN LIFE

Probably nowhere in the development of medical technological advances has our ability been greater than in the specific area of the prolongation or extension of human life almost at the will of the physician. The life-support systems which are available in almost any intensive care unit attest to this fact. It has always been far easier to exterminate life quite painlessly than to prolong it. The medical profession now has a two-edged sword: the extension of human life by artificial means and the painless termination of life by drugs. The ability of man to wield this sword has moral and ethical as well as practical considerations that are mind boggling.

Whenever a discussion centers around dying and the shortening of life, the antithesis of this, namely, the prolongation of life, must be considered. Technologically, medicine has advanced so quickly that older, unwritten understandings of "ordinary" and "extraordinary" care no longer seem applicable. What might have been considered "extraordinary" care a few years ago is now so commonplace as to be called "ordinary" (respirators, pacemakers, kidney dialysis machines, etc.). Furthermore, what starts off in a given case to be "ordinary" care such as the application of a respirator to a patient who is unable to breathe, turns out, when it becomes evident that the patient never can assume normal respirations on his own, to have been "extraordinary care," if one is permitted the liberty of changing the adjective after the fact. Perhaps an example would help to clarify this. If one were struck down by a car and had a serious head injury which rendered him unable to breathe and made him unable to respond, and if his bladder sphincter were in spasm so that he could not urinate, he could be placed on a respirator, he could be artificially fed intravenously or by a stomach tube, and his urinary obstruction could be taken care of by the proper placement of a catheter. If it were assumed that he would recover in a matter of a few days, all of these things would be "ordinary" care. If on the basis of superior knowledge of the neurosurgeon attending him at this time it were known that there was essentially no way he could be expected to recover, all of these things might be considered "extraordinary" care, since without them his injuries would produce death.

If one had acute appendicitis and postoperatively developed a situation where his kidneys did not function, to put him on a dialysis machine (an artificial kidney) which could handle his urinary function temporarily would be an extraordinary act and might at times be considered to be "extraordinary" care. However, in a vigorous, alert, productive individual with a normal life expectancy of several decades ahead of him, it should not be considered "extraordinary" care. On the other hand, if in a ninety-year-old individual the same kidney shutdown took place and was the result of a disease process that inevitably would take this patient's life, the institution of dialysis would be an "extraordinary procedure" and would definitely be thought of, by any medically competent individual, as providing "extraordinary" care. Here the difference perhaps is less difficult to ascertain than in the previously mentioned case of head injury.

To show how difficult predictions might be, *Medical World News* on May 5, 1974, reported a case of a woman with myasthenia gravis who lived "artificially" for 652 days in intensive care and then made a remarkable recovery. Said a hospital representative at the Harbor General Hospital in Torrance, California, "She made us recognize that there was no such thing as inordinate effort. She had such a tenacity for life we felt that everything we did, no matter how extraordinary, was appropriate to the situation."[1]

. . . [I]t is most difficult to judge medical action from the standpoint of what is legal justice alone. If one gets into the pure aspects of ethics, there could be concern that the use of a pain killer in a dying individual could so cloud his conscious response that he might not in his dying moments be in a position to make decisions which in theological terms might bear upon his eternal destiny. It is essentially impossible to control pain in most instances, particularly in a debilitated or dying individual, without at the same time temporarily impairing his ability to think. From a purely ethical point of view, because clouding of judgment accompanies relief from pain produced by drugs, the situation seems to be insurmountable and therefore has become acceptable.

With the technological advances in medicine, the opportunities for physician participation in momentous decisions concerning life and death increase dramatically. But so do the temptations to misuse this newfound expertise. The physician of a generation or two ago was practically powerless to extend life but on the other hand he faced fewer dilemmas. . . .

DILEMMAS FOR DOCTORS AND LAYMEN ALIKE

The dilemmas presented by euthanasia are not dilemmas for the medical profession alone. They are dilemmas for laymen as well. The situation is somewhat akin to the remarks that are made about the malpractice crisis in American medicine today. Many people say: "The doctors certainly have a difficult problem." The fact of the matter is that it is the patient who has a difficult problem. Who do you suppose will pay for the doctor's malpractice insurance premium which has increased in cost fivefold? You, the patient, will pay that. What other dangers exist for the patient in an era where the specter of malpractice suits hangs over the head of the responsible physician at all times? First of all, the physician will treat you not on the basis of what his experience and learned intuition dictates, but rather he will do those things which he feels would absolve him from eventual guilt were he ever sued, and he will neglect to do those things which you might need but which involve a high risk concerning a malpractice. In short, the patient's physician must practice defensive medicine and the loss is not only the physician's, it is the patient's.

So it is in the dilemmas surrounding euthanasia. Sooner or later you, the reader, will have to face some of these questions in reference to a member of your family and eventually your family will have to face these questions in reference to you. Indeed, you may be party to the latter dilemma as you approach the end of your life.

Once any category of human life is considered fair game in the arena of the right to life, where does it stop? If the mongoloid [Down's syndrome] is chosen as the first category whose life is not worthy to be lived, what about the blind and the deaf? If the hopeless cripple confined to a wheelchair and considered to be a burden on society is the first category to be chosen, what about the frail, the retarded, and the senile? It does not take much fanciful imagination to extend these categories to include certain categories of disease such as cystic fibrosis, diabetes, and a variety of neurologic disorders. The population-control people who are concerned about food supply have been very effective in influencing society's thinking on abortion; it seems very logical that eventually one of their targets could be the obese individual who not only has eaten too much already but has to eat a lot to sustain his large body.

It is very easy to slip into moral deception in a discussion of euthanasia. One starts from the point of view of abortion and says, "I can see why you are against abortion because after all someone, preferably the law, must protect the fetus because the fetus is not in a position to protect itself. But when one is talking of euthanasia, if the person is willing to undergo a 'mercy killing,' why should other people object?" The answer is really the same as it is for abortion. Abortion-on-demand opens up other abuses of which euthanasia is number one. Euthanasia opens up the opportunity at this early stage of the game for almost inconceivable fraud, deception, and deceit. Think of the burdensome elderly people, economically burdensome, whose rapid demise could be looked upon as an economic blessing for their family. Think of the temptation to hasten a legacy. Think of how easy, when there are ulterior motives, to emphasize the surcease from suffering and anxiety that comes with painless death.

PRACTICAL CONSIDERATIONS

I don't think a medical student is ever told what his mission in life is. Certainly no one told me when I was a medical student what was expected of me as a lifetime goal in assuming the role of a physician. Yet it is very clearly and indelibly imprinted upon the mind of the physician that the first obligation toward his patient is to heal him and cure him and to postpone death for as long a time as possible. The second goal is more difficult to enunciate and ever so much more difficult to practice: When cure is not possible the physician is to care for and comfort his dying patient. There is in here a gray area where the physician is not certain about the possibility of cure and yet is not ready to treat the patient as one who needs comfort in dying. The other side of that coin has to do with the behavior of the physician who, realizing that the opportunity for cure is passed, has two options: first, that of maintaining the life of a "dying" patient through the extremely difficult times of transition from active life to inactive life and from inactive life to death, or, secondly, to withhold certain supportive measures which would enable nature to take her course more quickly.

Let me illustrate. There is a unique tumor of childhood called the neuroblastoma in which I have been interested for more than thirty years. Because of this I have developed a broad clinical experience with the behavior of this tumor as it affects the lives of my patients and I have perhaps had more neuroblastoma patients referred to me than would normally be the case, because of my special interest in this tumor. I present this background in order to establish the fact that with this particular tumor I have considerable expertise in understanding the clinical course and have been able to predict with relative accuracy what will happen in a given patient when certain signs and symptoms occur or when certain responses to treatment are known. In a given situation I might have as a patient a five-year-old child whose tumor was diagnosed a year ago and who, in spite of all known treatment, has progressed to a place where although her primary tumor has been removed she now has recurrence of the tumor (metastases) in her bones. On the basis of everything I know by seeing scores of patients like her I know that her days of life are limited and that the longer she lives the more likely she is to have considerable pain. She might also become both deaf and blind, because those are sequelae that might be expected when this tumor spreads in the bones of the skull.

If this five-year-old youngster is quite anemic, her ability to understand what is happening to her might be clouded. If her normal hemoglobin level should be 12 and is now 6, I have two choices. I can let her exist with a deficient hemoglobin level knowing that it may shorten her life but also knowing that it will be beneficial in the sense that she will not be alert enough to understand all that is happening around her. On the other hand I could be a medical purist and give her blood transfusions until her hemoglobin level was up to acceptable standards. In the process of so doing she would become more alert, she would be more conscious of the things happening around her, she would feel her pain more deeply, and she might live longer to increase the problems presented by all of these things.

In the second place there are anticancer drugs which I know beyond any shadow of a doubt will not cure this child, but which may shrink the recurring tumor in several parts of her body, postponing the inevitable death by a matter of a few days or weeks. However, it is possible that the effect of these drugs will not be very dramatic on the tumors in the skull. They may relentlessly expand, producing blindness and deafness. Would it be better to let this little girl slip into death quietly, with relatively little pain, and with her parents knowing that she can both see and hear—or should we prolong her life by two or three weeks, increase the intensity and duration of the pain she would have, and possibly run the risk of the added terrible complications for the family to witness: blindness and/or deafness? In such a circumstance I opt to withhold supportive measures that would prolong miserable life for the patient to bear and the family to see.

I well remember the occasion on which I decided that this would always be my course of action in this particular tumor unless I was forced to do otherwise or there were some very extenuating circumstances. One of my patients was approaching the aforementioned condition and had been sent home because of the approach of the Christmas holidays and the desire of his family to have the child with them. In the days before his discharge I had promised him a chemistry set as a Christmas gift and on the day before Christmas I delivered the gift in the afternoon. His family took me into their living room and there before the Christmas tree was a big mound on the floor which looked like a heaped-up beige blanket. Under it was my patient on his hands and knees slumped down as though hands and knees could no longer support his weight. The story was most pitiful. Earlier he had asked to come down from his bedroom to see the electric trains under the Christmas tree and found a measure of comfort on his hands and knees before the trains. He asked not to be moved because he had found a position in which he seemed more comfortable than when lying in bed. He died the next day in that same position.

In a situation such as I have just described one gets to the very nonlegalistic moral core of the relationship of a physician with his patient. Whether the patient is a child and the relationship has to be with his parents or whether the patient is an adult and the physician's relationship must be with the patient himself and his relatives, there has to be a sense of trust and confidence that the physician will do the "right" thing whether the disease process is curable or is one which will cause death. There have been many occasions in my life when I have clearly described the thoughts that went through my mind as I outlined to parents why I planned what I did plan to do with their child. But much more often than that there has been between parent and physician an understanding which exceeds the bounds of pure trust and confidence, where the family seems to know, and I encourage them to think, that their child is in understanding hands as well as in competent hands, that their child will be kindly treated in this terrible process of dying to which death brings a sense of relief and release. Here the family senses that I will treat their child the way I would like someone in my position to treat my child were he in the same circumstance. Yet through all this there is the understanding that this life, waning though it may be, is precious to the patient, is precious to the family, is precious to me, and—in my particular belief—the understanding that this life is also precious to God.

Therefore, it should be very clear that the decisions that are made in any circumstance are tailored to the problems at hand, the background and experience if the physician, the depth of understanding of the family, and the relationship which exists between patient and physician and family and physician. There is no way that there can be a set of rules to govern this circumstance. Guidelines may be possible, but not rules. I can think of no more tragic circumstance to come upon the practice of medicine and no more tragic circumstance for a future patient to face than to have a legal decision made by someone in the field of jurisprudence who has not lived through these circumstances, and who could not in a lifetime of testimony understand what the problems are and how they should be handled. His training, his experience, and his emotions have not been intimately involved with similar circumstances in the past where his decision and his decision alone is the one that must answer all the questions, no matter how inadequately.

The arrival of the era of organ transplantation adds other series of dilemmas to the practice of medicine in reference to the ethics and the morality of the prolongation of life on the one hand or its extermination on the other. Add to all of the other questions that have been raised previously, the new one of terminating one life to make possible an organ transplant to another individual in order that the second individual's life may be meaningfully prolonged. Some of these decisions are relatively open and shut, as for example in brain death of an individual, perhaps young, who is kept alive by a respirator in the presence of a functioning heart. But one can also easily imagine the pressures that develop from the family of a patient consigned to death because of the lack of a vital organ, when the patient could have his life significantly prolonged by the removal of that organ from another individual whose life may not be considered by the patient and other interested parties to be worthy of extraordinary care. These pressures are felt especially by those engaged in kidney transplant programs. . . .

THEOLOGY, MORALITY, AND ETHICS

Although the termination of unborn life precludes the living of the life for threescore and ten years, whereas euthanasia only shortens a life that has already been lived, this is no reason to regard the taking of a life by euthanasia as any less serious a moral decision than that by abortion.

Obviously, the great majority of people realize that a decision concerning abortion will never be theirs to make personally. It naturally follows that many people will be indifferent to the implications of liberalized abortion laws, not recognizing how the change in our understanding of abortion affects so many other aspects of our lives today and in the future. But when it comes to death, there is no one who can say that a decision concerning the way his death is managed will be of no concern to him. The death rate is still one per capita.

It has always been of considerable interest to me that any discussion of human life rapidly and inevitably becomes associated with theological discussions. The fact that as distinguished a journal as the *Human Life Review* would contain technical articles on population, learned discourses on jurisprudence, and publish them side by side with the theological implications of man's regard for human life suggests to me incontrovertibly that life and death are God's business.

As with abortion, any discussion of euthanasia by the individual leans heavily upon that individual's understanding of the sanctity or lack of sanctity of human life, upon an understanding of man's understanding of God, and upon whether or not in the synthesis of these things the individual believes that there is life not worthy to be lived. My own perspective of the dilemmas presented by euthanasia represent an understanding produced by the synthesis of where my belief in biblical revelation crosses my experience in medicine.

Each reader . . . must face the fact that his own beliefs on these matters may be based on theological arguments of which he is not aware, as well as on Christian spinoffs that regulate society.

To one raised in Judeo-Christian moral philosophy, life might be considered on a much higher plane than the right considered inalienable by Thomas Jefferson. If one considers life as a sacred privilege, that understanding can be extended to include the view that this sacred privilege was indeed designed by God in order that a creature might relate to the Creator in a personal way—in a relationship in which God is sovereign.

If man was indeed created in the image of God and he was created for a life of fellowship with God, then death is alien to anything that God in his creation of man intended before man's fall. From a theological point of view the sanctity of life represents, or rather understands, man as a trinity: he is a soul, he does inhabit a body, and he has a spirit. In the trinitarian Christian view there is a sanctity of life for each of these.

The term "death with dignity" has caught on because of its alliterative catchiness rather than because it represents anything based upon Judeo-Christian moral principles.[2] The Judeo-Christian understanding of the fall of man is essential to an appreciation of this point of view. Man was created in the image of God and would have lived in fellowship with Him, had it not been for the disobedience of the progenitor of our race, Adam. Anything that exists within man's nature to enable him to have fellowship with God must be regarded as a gift from God and, in a sense, the worthiness of this life has meaning only insofar as it has this relationship to God.

In a sense the whole problem of the right to live and the right to die, centering around one's understanding of abortion and euthanasia, has a significant analogy to the behavior of Lucifer. We do not know whence his temptation came but we do know that he sought to be "like the most high."[3] Our society, having lost its understanding of the sanctity of human life, is pushing the medical profession into assuming one of God's prerogatives, namely, deciding what life shall be born and when life should end.

A great deal of our Western civilization with its concomitant culture is based upon Christian principles, Christian ethics, Christian morality. Even though many refer to this era as the post-Christian era, there are a remarkable number of spinoffs that we accept as everyday rights and privileges which would never have been part of Western society except for Christian influence.

If one were to superimpose a map of the Western world showing those places where the Christian gospel has been preached, where Christian morality and influence has had its greatest impact, upon another map showing those parts of the Western world where what used to be called social reforms were most prevalent—literacy, education, hospitals, orphanages, homes for the aged, institutions for the retarded and the insane available to all regardless of creed—these maps would be almost identical.

Without theological insights that help to form the basis of one's understanding of matters relating to the life and death of patients, I would find it impossible to make judgments in these matters. I suspect that theological principles, some of which may be vague implantations from early religious training, are probably at work in the minds of the great majority of physicians as they face some of these decisions.

If there is not to be a Judeo-Christian ethic in the preservation of life in matters relating to euthanasia, what does the future hold? To assume the role of prophet, I can almost hear the arguments that will be given by the proponents of euthanasia outlining the safeguards that the state can build into euthanasia laws to prevent euthanasia from becoming perverted as it once was in the days of the Nazis in Germany. It comes down to the question as it does in reference to any matter of life: "Is there life not worthy to be lived?" The day may come when a death selection committee may objectively consider my life not to be worth much. On the other hand the subjective worth of my life in my eyes and those in my family who love me might be quite different. Many cases will be open and shut, but the number of cases in the gray area will exceed those where physicians have clarity of thought and relative unanimity of opinion. Certainly the rights of individuals will disappear; depersonalization and dehumanization will reign. If our human-value concepts are to be preserved, no one should take the life of another human being even passively without the deepest concern and consideration of all the attendant implications. Once the human-value ethic becomes weakened or tarnished, it doesn't take long for inhuman experimentation on human bodies to take place. Auchwitz could be in the offing.

WHERE DO WE GO FROM HERE?

The decision of the Supreme Court in favor of abortion on demand literally hands over the decision on the survival of one person's life to another person. All of the economic, social, emotional, and compassionate arguments that are used in favor of abortion very suddenly become the same arguments for euthanasia.

It does not take long to move rapidly to a new set of standards once we have learned to live for a short time with an abrogation of a former principle. Take the medical profession, for example. For four centuries longer than the Christian era, doctors have taken the Hippocratic oath. To be sure, there are many things that are outdated because of the difference in culture between the time of Hippocrates and this modern era. To be sure, there are changes in our understanding of modern medicine which alter or render obsolete certain areas of the Hippocratic oath. But the one thing that the public could rely on was that the medical profession, functioning on the traditional oath of Hippocrates, was in the business of being on the side of life. Life was to be preserved just as suffering was to be alleviated. But nowhere were the skills of the physician to be used as intervention to lower the health standards of the patient or to shorten his life.

If the medical profession abandons the life principle embodied in the Hippocratic oath and sees its privilege to extend to the interruption of unborn life in the womb and to painlessly exterminate a waning life much as the veterinarian would put an ailing dog to sleep, it will have changed its *raison d'être*. The patient can no longer look at his physician as his advocate for the extension of life—because when in the mind of that physician that patient's life is waning, the sick person has no guarantee that the physician will approach him in the role of life preserver; he may be coming as executioner. The medical profession has been disappointingly silent as they have heard the intellectual arguments, Supreme Court rulings, and population-concern pressures that have begun to alter the fundamental basis which has for so long set them apart as the proponents of the healing art.

Before the century is out, it is quite possible that the elderly will exceed in numbers those who bear the burden of their support, whether as family or under some legal technicality such as the Social Security Act. If the question of euthanasia presents a dilemma now, on moral and ethical grounds, think of what it will present in days to come when, in addition to moral and ethical considerations, there is the overpowering question of economics. Unless we get our ethics and our morals straightened out now, the death selection committee that decides for you may be motivated more by money than by ecological concerns.

Most of the dilemmas that present themselves in reference to the dying patient have been described. If the reader feels at this juncture that he does not have a good grasp of how the author would act in every imaginable circumstance, then the reader has grasped the situation rather well. It is almost impossible to present in capsule form how one feels on this subject, so extenuating are the circumstances in different situations. Perhaps no more difficult question is ever asked of me by an intern or a resident than to summarize in a few sentences my feelings on this subject. When asked to do so, I put it somewhat like this: "As a basic principle, keep as many men at as many guns for as long a time as possible; that's how you win the war. I am in the life-saving business and that comes first, but I recognize also that I am in the business of alleviating suffering. I never take a deliberate action with the motive of terminating a patient's life. It is possible that a patient's life might be shortened by some therapeutic measure I employ with the intent of relieving suffering. In some circumstances where I believe that I have sufficient experience and expertise with the life history of a disease process and my patient's response to that disease as well as to his therapy, I might withhold treatment that could be considered extraordinary or heroic in the given circumstance in reference to the quality of life that might be salvaged for a short period of time." Even as I write these words I recognize full well the chance for errors in judgment. Because of that I try to err only on the side of life.

NOTES

1. *Medical World News* (May 5, 1974).

2. Editorial, *The Philadelphia Inquirer* (November 12, 1975). William A. Reusher, Op-Ed page, *The Philadelphia Inquirer* (November 23, 1975).

3. Isaiah 14:14.

10

Sanctity of Life versus Quality of Life

Joseph Fletcher

It is harder morally to justify letting somebody die a slow and ugly death, dehumanized, than it is to justify helping him to escape from such misery. This is the case at least in any code of ethics which is humanistic or personalistic, i.e., in any code of ethics which has a value system that puts humanness and personal integrity above biological life and function. It makes no difference whether such an ethics system is grounded in a theistic or a naturalistic philosophy. We may believe that God wills human happiness or that man's happiness is, as Protagoras thought, a self-validating standard of the good and the right. But what counts *ethically* is whether human needs come first—not whether the ultimate sanction is transcendental or secular.

What follows is a moral defense of human initiatives in death and dying. Primarily I mean active or direct euthanasia, which helps the patient to die, not merely the passive or indirect form of euthanasia which "lets the patient go" by simply withholding life-preserving treatments. The plain fact is that indirect or negative euthanasia is already a *fait accompli* in modern medicine. Every day in a hundred hospitals across the land decisions are made clinically that the line has been crossed from prolonging genuinely human life to only prolonging

From "Euthanasia," in *Humanhood: Essays in Biomedical Ethics* (Buffalo, N.Y.: Prometheus Books, 1979), pp. 149–158. Copyright 1979 by Joseph Fletcher.

subhuman dying; and when that judgment is made, respirators are turned off, life-perpetuating intravenous infusions stopped, proposed surgery canceled, and drugs countermanded. So-called Code 90 stickers are put on many record-jackets, indicating "Give no intensive care or resuscitation." Arguing pro and con about negative euthanasia is therefore merely flogging a dead horse. Ethically, the issue whether we may let the patient go is as dead as Queen Anne.

Straight across the board of religious traditions there is substantial agreement that we are not morally obligated to preserve life in *all* terminal cases. (The religious-ethical defense of negative euthanasia is far more generally accepted by ministers, priests, and rabbis than medical people recognize or as yet even accept.) Humanist morality shows the same nonabsolutistic attitude about preserving life. Indeed, not only Protestant, Catholic, and Jewish teaching take this stance; it is also true of Buddhist, Hindu, and Moslem ethics. In short, the claim that we ought always to do everything we can to preserve any patient's life as long as possible is now discredited. The last serious advocate of this unconditional provitalist doctrine was David Karnofsky, the great tumor research scientist of the Sloan-Kettering Institute in New York. The issue about *negative* (indirect) euthanasia is settled ethically.

Given modern medicine's capabilities, always to do what is technically possible to prolong life would be morally indefensible on any ground other than a vitalistic outlook. That is, the opinion that biological survival is the first-order value and that all other considerations, such as personality, dignity, well-being, and self-possession, necessarily take second place. Vestigial last-ditch provitalists still mumble threateningly about "what the Nazis did," but in fact the Nazis never engaged in euthanasia or mercy killing. What they did was merciless killing, either for genocidal or ruthless experimental purposes.

One way of putting this is to say that the traditional ethics based on the sanctity of life, which was the classical doctrine of medical idealism in its prescientific phases, must give way to an ethics of the *quality* of life. This comes about for humane reasons. It is a result of modern medicine's successes, not failures. "New occasions teach new duties, time makes ancient good uncouth," as Whittier said.

There are many pre-ethical or metaethical issues that are often overlooked in ethical discussions. People of equally good reasoning powers and a high respect for the rules on inference will still puzzle and even infuriate each other. This is because they fail to see that their moral judgments proceed from significantly different values, ideals, and starting points. If God's will (perhaps "specially revealed" in the Bible or "generally revealed" in his Creation) is against any responsible human initiative in the dying process, or if sheer life is believed to be, as such, more desirable than anything else, then those who hold these opinions will not find much merit in any case we might make for either kind of euthanasia, direct or indirect. If, on the other hand, the highest good is personal integrity and human well-being, then euthanasia in either form could or might be the right thing, depending on the situation. This latter kind of ethics is the key to what will be said in this chapter.

Let's say it again, clearly, for the sake of truly serious ethical discourse. Many of us look upon living and dying as we do upon health and medical care, as person-centered. This is not a solely or basically biological understanding of what it means to be "alive" and to be "dead." It asserts that a so-called vegetable, the brain-damaged victim of an auto accident or a microcephalic newborn or a case of massive neurologic deficit and lost cerebral capacity, who nevertheless goes on breathing and whose midbrain or brain stem continues to support spontaneous organ functions, is in such a situation no longer a human being, no longer a person, no longer really alive. It is *personal* function that counts, not biological function. Humanness is understood as primarily rational, not physiological. This "doctrine of man" puts the *homo* and *ratio* before the *vita*. It holds that being human is more valuable than being alive.

All of this is said just to make it clear from the outset that biomedical progress is forcing us, whether we welcome it or not, to make fundamental *conceptual* changes as well as scientific and medical changes. Not only are the conditions of life and death changing, because of our greater control and, in consequence, our greater decision-making responsibility; our *definitions* of life and death also have to change to keep pace with the new realities.

These changes are signaled in a famous surgeon's remark recently: "When the brain is gone there is no point in keeping anything else going." What he meant was that with an end of cerebration, i.e., the function of the cerebral cortex, the *person* is gone (dead) no matter how many other spontaneous or artificially supported functions persist in the heart, lungs, and vascular system. Such noncerebral processes might as well be turned off, whether they are natural or artificial.

This conclusion is of great philosophical and religious interest because it reaffirms the ancient Christian-European belief that the core of humanness, of the *humanum,* lies in the *ratio*—man's rational faculty. It is not the loss of brain function in general but of cerebral function (the synthesizing "mind") in particular that establishes that death has ensued.

Using the old conventional conceptual apparatus, we naturally thought about both life and death as events, not as processes, which, of course, they are. We supposed that these events or episodes depended on the accidents of nature or on some kind of special providence. It is therefore no surprise to hear people grumbling that a lot of the decision making that has to be carried out in modern medical care is playing God. And given that way of thinking, the only possible answer to the charge is to accept it: Yes, we *are* playing God. But the real question is: Which or whose God are we playing?

In their growing up spiritually, men are now turning to a "God" who or which is the creative principle behind things—behind the test tube as much as behind the earthquake and volcano. This can be believed, but the old God's sacralistic inhibitions on human freedom and research can no longer be submitted to.

We must rid ourselves of that obsolete theodicy according to which God is not only the cause but also the builder of nature and its works, and not only the builder but even the manager. That archaic view made God himself the efficient as well as the final cause of earthquake and fire, of life and death, and by logical inference any interference with nature (which is exactly what medicine is) was impious. Ethically, it was unresponsible.

Most of our major moral problems are posed by scientific discoveries and by the subsequent technical know-how we gain, in the control of life and health and death. Ethical questions jump out at us from every laboratory and clinic. May we exercise these controls at all, we wonder—and if so, then when, where, how? Every advance in medical capabilities is an increase in our moral responsibility, a widening of the range of our decision-making obligations.

Genetics, molecular biology, fetology, and obstetrics have developed to a point where we now have effective control over the start of human life's continuum. From now on it would be irresponsible to leave baby making to mere chance and impulse, as we once *had* to do.

What has taken place in birth control is equally imperative in death control. The whole armory of resuscitation and prolongation of life forces us to be responsible decision makers about death as much as about birth; there must be quality control in the terminating of life as in its initiating. It is ridiculous to give ethical approval to the positive ending of subhuman life *in utero,* as we do in therapeutic abortions for reasons of mercy and compassion, but refuse to approve of positively ending a subhuman life *in extremis.* If we are morally obliged to put an end to a pregancy when an amniocentesis reveals a terribly defective fetus, we are equally obliged to put an end to a patient's hopeless misery when a brain scan reveals that a patient with cancer has advanced brain metastases.

Only man is aware of death. Animals know pain, and fear it, but not death. Furthermore, in humans the ability to meet death and even to regard it sometimes as a friend is a sign of manliness. But in the new patterns of medicine and health care patients tend to die in a moribund or comatose state, so that death comes without the patient's knowledge. The Elizabethan litany's petition, ". . . from sudden death, good Lord, deliver us," has become irrelevant much if not most of the time.

It is because of this incompetent condition of so many of the dying that we cannot discuss the ethical issues of elective death only in the narrow terms of voluntary, patient-chosen euthanasia. A careful typology of elective death will distinguish at least five forms— five ways of dying which are not willy-nilly blind chance but matters of choice, purpose, and responsible freedom. (Historical ethics and moral theology are obviously major sources of suggestion for these distinctions.)

ACTIVE, VOLUNTARY, DIRECT

This is death chosen and carried out by the patient. The most familiar way is the overdose left near at hand for the patient. It is a matter of simple request and of personal liberty. In a word, it is suicide. In any particular case, we might properly raise the question of the patient's competence, but to hold that euthanasia in this category is justifiable entails a rejection of the simplistic canard that all suicides are mentally disordered.

Presumably a related issue arises around the conventional notion of consent in medical ethics. The codes (American Medical Association, Helsinki, World Medical Association, Nuremberg) all contend that valid consent to any surgery or treatment requires a reasonable prospect of benefit to the patient. What, then, is benefit? Could death in some situations be a benefit? As a question in the relativity of values, my own answer is in the affirmative.

PASSIVE, VOLUNTARY, DIRECT

The choice might be made either *in situ* or long in advance of a terminal illness, e.g., by exacting a promise that if and when Shakespeare's "bare bodkin" or potion cannot be self-administered, somebody will do it for the patient. In this case the patient gives to others—physicians, lawyers, family, friends—the discretion to end it all as and when the situation requires, if the patient becomes comatose or too dysfunctioned to take the necessary steps himself.

PASSIVE, VOLUNTARY, INDIRECT

This, like the second form, is done for, rather than by, the patient, but with his consent and by indirect means only, not directly. A directive or form called the Living Will is in wide use, with legal enforcement in some states (but not all). For example, in these right-to-die laws the recorded wish of a comatose or suffering patient (if, and only if, the patient is terminally ill) is protected from those who would disregard the patient's directive to have all treatment stopped. Hospital staff, physicians, and family often try to do this. As people learn to fear senescence more than death (a fear brought about by undiscriminating resuscitation practices), this policy spreads. Neither the common law tradition nor statute law is equipped to deal with the anti-euthanasia culture-lag. (In Italy, Germany, and Switzerland the law provides for a reduction of penalties when it is done at the patient's request.)

PASSIVE, INVOLUNTARY, DIRECT

This is the form or procedure in which a simple "mercy killing" is done on a patient's behalf without his present or prior consent. Instances would be when an idiot is given a fatal dose, or the death of a child in the worst stages of Tay-Sachs disease is speeded along, or when a man trapped inextricably in a blazing fire is shot to end his suffering, or a shutdown is ordered on a patient deep in a mindless condition, irreversibly, perhaps due to an injury or an infection or some biological breakdown. It is this form of euthanasia which has posed the problem several times in court trials and indictments. . . .

PASSIVE, INVOLUNTARY, INDIRECT

This is the "letting the patient go" tactic which is being acted out every day in our hospitals. Nothing is done for the patient positively to release him from his tragic condition (other than "trying to make him comfortable"). What is done is done *for* him rather than in response to any request by him. It is an uninstructed proxy decision. As we all know, even this passive policy of compassion is followed only grudgingly, much of the time. It continues to be at least theoretically vulnerable to malpractice and criminal-neglect suits under the lagging law—brought, possibly, by angry or venal members of the family or litigious lawyers.

Ethically regarded, however, this euthanasia practice is manifestly superficial, morally timid, and evasive of the real issue. I repeat: it is harder morally to justify letting somebody die a slow and ugly death, dehumanized, than it is to justify helping him to avoid it.

What, then, is the real issue? In a few words, it is whether we can morally justify taking it into our own hands, as human beings, to hasten death for ourselves (suicide) or for others (mercy killing) out of reasons of compassion. The answer in my view is clearly yes, on both sides of it. Indeed, *to justify either one, suicide or mercy killing, is to justify the other.*

The heart of the matter analytically is the question of whether the end justifies the means. If the end sought is the patient's death as a release from pointless misery and dehumanization, then the requisite or appropriate means is justified. The old maxim of some moral theologians was *finis sanctificat media.* The point is that no act is anything but random and *meaningless* unless it is purposefully related to some end or object. To be moral an act must be seeking an end. However, to hold that the end justifies the means does not entail the absurd notion that *any* means can be justified by *any* end. The priority of the end is paired with the principle of 'proportionate good'; any disvalue in the means must be outweighed by the value gained in the end. In systems analysis, with its pragmatic approach, the language would be: the benefit must repay the cost or the trade-off is not justified. It comes down to this, that in some situations a morally good end can justify a relatively bad means, on the principle of proportionate good.

The really searching question of conscience is, therefore, whether we are right in believing that *the well-being of persons* is the highest good. If so, then it follows that either suicide or mercy killing could be the right thing to do in some exigent and tragic circumstances. This could be the case, for instance, when an incorrigible human vegetable, whether spontaneously functioning or artificially supported, is progressively degraded while constantly eating up private or public financial resources in violation of the distributive justice owed to others. In such cases the patient is actually already departed and only his body is left, and the needs of others have a stronger claim upon us morally. The fair allocation of scarce resources is as profound an ethical obligation as any we can imagine in a civilized society, and it arises very practically at the clinical level when triage officers make their decisions at the expense of some patients' needs in favor of others'.

Another way of putting this is to say that the crucial question is not whether the end justifies the means (what else could?) but *what justifies the end?* And this chapter's answer is, plainly and confidently, that human happiness and well-being is the highest good or *summum bonum,* and that therefore any ends or purposes which that standard or ideal validates are just, right, good. This is what humanistic medicine is all about; it is what the concepts of loving concern and social justice are built upon.

This position comes down to the belief that our moral acts, including suicide and mercy killing, are right or wrong depending on the consequences aimed at (we sometimes fail, of course, through ignorance or poor reasoning), and that the consequences are good or evil according to whether and how much they serve human values. This is precisely a "consequential" moral judgment.

I believe that this mode of ethics is both implicit and explicit in the morality of medical care and biomedical research. Its reasoning is inductive, not deductive, and it proceeds empirically from the data of each actual case or problem, choosing the course that offers an optimum or maximum of desired consequences. Medicine is not *a prioristic* or *prejudiced* in its ethos and modalities, and therefore to proscribe either suicide or mercy killing is so blatantly nonconsequential that it calls for critical scrutiny. It fails to make sense. It is unclinical and doctrinaire.

The problem exists because of the other kind of ethics which holds that we ought or ought not to do certain things no matter how good or bad the consequences might foreseeably be. Such rules are prohibitions or taboos, expressed as thou-shalt-nots. While my ethics is teleological or end-oriented, the opposite approach is *deontological* (from the Greek *deonteis,* meaning duty); i.e., it is duty-ethics, not goal-ethics. Its advocates sometimes sneer at any determination of obligation in terms of consequences, calling it "a mere morality of goals."

In duty-ethics what is right is whatever act obeys or adheres to the rules, even though the foreseeable result will be inhumane. That is, its highest good is not human happiness and well-being but obedience to a rule—or what we might call a prejudiced or predetermined decision based not on the clinical variables but on some transcending "principle."

For example, the fifth of the Ten Commandments, which prohibits killing, is cited as a strict prohibition for nonconsequentialists when it comes to killing in the service of humane values like mercy and compassion, and yet at the same time they ignore their "moral law" when it comes to self-defense. The egocentricity and solipsism in this moral posture, which is a very common one, never ceases to bemuse consequentialists. You may end your neighbor's life for your own sake, but you may not do it for his sake! And you may end your own life for your neighbor's sake, as in an act of sacrificial heroism, but you may not end your life for your own sake. This is a veritable mare's nest of nonsense!

The plain hard logic of it is that the end or purpose of both negative and positive euthanasia is exactly the same: to contrive or bring about the patient's death. Acts of deliberate omission are morally not different from acts of commission. But in the Anglo-American *law,* it is a crime to push a blind man off a cliff. It is not, however, a crime to deliberately not lift a finger to prevent his walking over the edge. This is an unpleasant feature of legal reasoning which is alien to ethics and to a sensitive conscience. Ashamed of it, even the courts fall back on such legal fictions as insanity in euthanasia cases, and this has the predictable effect of undermining our respect for the law.

There is something obviously evasive when we rule motive out in charging people with the crime of mercy killing, but then bring it back in again for purposes of determining punishment! It is also a menacing delimitation of the concepts of culpability, responsibility, and negligence. No *ethically* disciplined decision maker could so blandly separate right and wrong from motives, foresight, and consequences. (Be it noted, however, that motive is taken into account in German and Swiss law, and that several European countries provide for recognition of "homicide when requested" as a special category.)

It is naive and superficial to suppose that because we don't do anything positively to hasten a patient's death we have thereby avoided complicity in his death. Not doing anything is doing something; it is a decision to act every bit as much as deciding for any other deed. If I decide not to eat or drink any more, knowing what the consequence will be, I have committed suicide as surely as if I had used a gas oven. If physicians decide not to open an imperforate anus in a severe 21-trisomy newborn, they have committed mercy killing as surely as if they had used a poison pellet!

Let the reader at this point now ask himself once more if he is a consequentialist or an *a priori* decision maker; and again, let him ask himself if he is a humanist or alternatively has something he holds to be better than the well-being of human beings. (Thoughtless religious people will sometimes point out that we are required to love God as well as our neighbors, but can the two loves ever come into conflict? Actually, is there any way to love God other than through the neighbor? Only mystics imagine that they can love God directly and discretely.)

Occasionally I hear a physician say that he could not bring himself to resort to direct euthanasia. That may be so. What anybody would do in such tragic situations is a problem in psychology, however, not in ethics. We are not asking what we would do but what we *should* do. Any of us who has an intimate knowledge of what happens in terminal illnesses can tell stories of rational people—both physicians and family—who were quite clear ethically about the rightness of an overdose or of "turning off the machine," and yet found themselves too inhibited to give the word or do the deed. That is a phenomenon of primary interest to psychology, and of only incidental interest to ethics.

Careful study of the best texts of the Hippocratic Oath shows that it says nothing at all about preserving life, as such. It says that "so far as power and discernment shall be mine, I will carry out regimen for the benefit of the sick and will keep them from harm and wrong." The case for euthanasia depends upon how we understand "benefit of the sick" and "harm" and "wrong." If we regard de-humanized and merely biological life as sometimes real harm and the very opposite of benefit, to refuse to welcome or even introduce death would be quite wrong morally.

In most states in this country people now can, and do, carry cards, legally enforceable, which explain the carrier's wish that when he dies his organs and tissue should be used for transplant when needed by the living. The day will come when people will also be able to carry a card, notarized and legally executed, which explains that they do not want to be kept alive beyond the *humanum* point, and authorizing the ending of their biological processes by any of the methods of euthanasia which seems appropriate. . . . Suicide may or may not be the ultimate problem of philosophy, as Albert Camus thought it is, but in any case it is the ultimate problem of medical ethics.

11

The Wrongfulness of Euthanasia

J. Gay-Williams

My impression is that euthanasia—the idea, if not the practice—is slowly gaining acceptance within our society. Cynics might attribute this to an increasing tendency to devalue human life, but I do not believe this is the major factor. The acceptance is much more likely to be the result of unthinking sympathy and benevolence. Well-publicized, tragic stories like that of Karen Quinlan elicit from us deep feelings of compassion. We think to ourselves, "She and her family would be better off if she were dead." It is an easy step from this very human response to the view that if someone (and others) would be better off dead, then it must be all right to kill that person.[1] Although I respect the compassion that leads to this conclusion, I believe the conclusion is wrong. I want to show that euthanasia is wrong. It is inherently wrong, but it is also wrong judged from the standpoints of self-interest and of practical effects.

Before presenting my arguments to support this claim, it would be well to define "euthanasia." An essential aspect of euthanasia is that it involves taking a human life, either one's own or that of another. Also, the person whose life is taken must be someone who is believed to be suffering from some disease or injury from which recovery cannot reasonably be expected. Finally, the action must be deliberate and intentional. Thus, euthanasia is intentionally taking the life of a presumably hopeless person. Whether the life is one's own or that of another, the taking of it is still euthanasia.

It is important to be clear about the deliberate and intentional aspect of the killing. If a hopeless person is given an injection of the wrong drug by mistake and this causes his death, this is wrongful killing but not euthanasia. The killing cannot be the result of an accident. Furthermore, if the person is given an injection of a drug that is believed to be necessary to treat his disease or better his condition and the person dies as a result, then this is neither wrongful killing nor euthanasia. The intention was to make the patient well, not kill him. Similarly, when a patient's condition is such that it is not reasonable to hope that any medical procedures or treatments will save his life, a failure to implement the procedures or treatments is not euthanasia. If the person dies, this will be as a result of his injuries or disease and not because of his failure to receive treatment.

The failure to continue treatment after it has been realized that the patient has little chance of benefitting from it has been characterized by some as "passive euthanasia." This phrase is misleading and mistaken.[2] In such cases, the person involved is not killed (the first essential aspect of euthanasia), nor is the death of the person intended by the withholding of additional treatment (the third essential aspect of euthanasia). The aim may be to spare the person additional and unjustifiable pain, to save him from the indignities of hopeless manipulations, and to avoid increasing the financial and emotional burdens on his family. When I buy a pencil it is so that I can use it to write, not to contribute to an increase in the gross national product. This may be an unintended consequence of my action, but it is not the aim of my action. So it is with failing to continue the treatment of a dying person. I intend his death no more than I intend to reduce the GNP by not using medical supplies. His is an unintended dying, and so-called "passive euthanasia" is not euthanasia at all.

THE ARGUMENT FROM NATURE

Every human being has a natural inclination to continue living. Our reflexes and responses fit us to fight attackers, flee wild animals, and dodge out of the way of trucks. In our daily lives we exercise the caution and care necessary to protect ourselves. Our bodies are similarly structured for survival right down to the molecular level. When we are cut, our capillaries seal shut, our blood clots, and fibrogen is produced to start the process of healing the wound. When we are invaded by bacteria, antibodies are produced to fight against the alien organisms, and their remains are swept out of the body by special cells designed for clean-up work.

Euthanasia does violence to this natural goal of survival. It is literally acting against nature because all the processes of nature are bent towards the end of bodily survival. Euthanasia defeats these subtle mechanisms in a way that, in a particular case, disease and injury might not.

It is possible, but not necessary, to make an appeal to revealed religion in this connection.[3] Man as trustee of his body acts against God, its rightful possessor, when he takes his own life. He also violates the commandment to hold life sacred and never to take it without just and compelling cause. But since this appeal will persuade only those who are prepared to accept that religion has access to revealed truths, I shall not employ this line of argument.

It is enough, I believe, to recognize that the organization of the human body and our patterns of behavioral responses make the continuation of life a natural goal. By reason alone, then, we can recognize that euthanasia sets us against our own nature.[4] Furthermore, in doing so, euthanasia does violence to our dignity. Our dignity comes from seeking our ends. When one of our goals is survival, and actions are taken that eliminate that goal, then our natural dignity suffers. Unlike animals, we are conscious through reason of our nature and our ends. Euthanasia involves acting as if this dual nature—inclination towards survival and awareness of this as an end—did not exist. Thus, euthanasia denies our basic human character and requires that we regard ourselves or others as something less than fully human.

THE ARGUMENT FROM SELF-INTEREST

The above arguments are, I believe, sufficient to show that euthanasia is inherently wrong. But there are reasons for considering it wrong when judged by standards other than reason. Because death is final and irreversible, euthanasia contains within it the possibility that we will work against our own interest if we practice it or allow it to be practiced on us.

Contemporary medicine has high standards of excellence and a proven record of accomplishment, but it does not possess perfect and complete knowledge. A mistaken diagnosis is possible, and so is a mistaken prognosis. Consequently, we may believe that we are dying of a disease when, as a matter of fact, we may not be. We may think that we have no hope of recovery when, as a matter of fact, our chances are quite good. In such circumstances, if euthanasia were permitted, we would die needlessly. Death is final and the chance of error too great to approve the practice of euthanasia.

Also, there is always the possibility that an experimental procedure or a hitherto untried technique will pull us through. We should at least keep this option open, but euthanasia closes it off. Furthermore, spontaneous remission does occur in many cases. For no apparent reason, a patient simply recovers when those all around him, including his physicians, expected him to die. Euthanasia would just guarantee their expectations and leave no room for the "miraculous" recoveries that frequently occur.

Finally, knowing that we can take our life at any time (or ask another to take it) might well incline us to give up too easily. The will to live is strong in all of us, but it can be weakened by pain and suffering and feelings of hopelessness. If during a bad time we allow ourselves to be killed, we never have a chance to reconsider. Recovery from a serious illness requires that we fight for it, and anything that weakens our determination by suggesting that there is an easy way out is ultimately against our own interest. Also, we may be inclined towards euthanasia because of our concern for others. If we see our sickness and suffering as an emotional and financial burden on our family, we may feel that to leave our life is to make their lives easier.[5] The very presence of the possibility of euthanasia may keep us from surviving when we might.

THE ARGUMENT FROM PRACTICAL EFFECTS

Doctors and nurses are, for the most part, totally committed to saving lives. A life lost is, for them, almost a personal failure, an insult to their skills and knowledge. Euthanasia as a practice might well alter this. It could have a corrupting influence so that in any case that is severe doctors and nurses might not try hard enough to save the patient. They might decide that the patient would simply be "better off dead" and take the steps necessary to make that come about. This attitude could then carry over to their dealings with patients less seriously ill. The result would be an overall decline in the quality of medical care.

Finally, euthanasia as a policy is a slippery slope. A person apparently hopelessly ill may be allowed to take his own life. Then he may be permitted to deputize others to do it for him should he no longer be able to act. The judgment of others then becomes the ruling factor. Already at this point euthanasia is not personal and voluntary, for others are acting "on behalf of" the patient as they see fit. This may well incline them to act on behalf of other patients who have not authorized them to exercise their judgment. It is only a short step, then, from voluntary euthanasia (self-inflicted or authorized), to directed euthanasia administered to a patient who has given no authorization, to involuntary euthanasia conducted as part of a social policy.[6] Recently many psychiatrists and sociologists have argued that we define as "mental illness" those forms of behavior that we disapprove of.[7] This gives us license then to lock up those who display the behavior. The category of the "hopelessly ill" provides the possibility of even worse abuse. Embedded in a social policy, it would give society or its representatives the authority to eliminate all those who might be considered too "ill" to function normally any longer. The dangers of euthanasia are too great to all to run the risk of approving it in any form. The first slippery step may well lead to a serious and harmful fall.

I hope that I have succeeded in showing why the benevolence that inclines us to give approval of euthanasia is misplaced. Euthanasia is inherently wrong because it violates the nature and dignity of human beings. But even those who are not convinced by this must be persuaded that the potential personal and social dangers inherent in euthanasia are sufficient to forbid our approving it either as a personal practice or as a public policy.

Suffering is surely a terrible thing, and we have a clear duty to comfort those in need and to ease their suffering when we can. But suffering is also a natural part of life with values for the individual and for others that we should not overlook. We may legitimately seek for others and for ourselves an easeful death, as Arthur Dyck has pointed out.[8] Euthanasia, however, is not just an easeful death. It is a wrongful death. Euthanasia is not just dying. It is killing.

NOTES

1. For a more sophisticated defense of this position see Philippa Foot, "Euthanasia," *Philosophy and Public Affairs* 6 (1977): 85-112. Foot does not endorse the radical conclusion that euthanasia, voluntary and involuntary, is always right.

2. James Rachels rejects the distinction between active and passive euthanasia as morally irrelevant in his "Active and Passive Euthanasia," *The New England Journal of Medicine* 292 (January 9, 1975): 78-80 (see this volume, chapter 6). But see the criticism by Foot, *Philosophy and Public Affairs,* pp. 100-103.

3. For a defense of this view, see J. V. Sullivan, "The Immorality of Euthanasia," in *Beneficent Euthanasia,* edited by Marvin Kohl (Buffalo, N.Y.: Prometheus Books, 1975), pp. 34-44.

4. This point is made by Ray V. McIntyre in "Voluntary Euthanasia: The Ultimate Perversion," *Medical Counterpoint,* vol. 2, pp. 26-29.

5. Ibid., p. 28.

6. See Sullivan, op. cit., for a fuller argument in support of this view.

7. See, for example, Thomas S. Szasz, *The Myth of Mental Illness,* rev. ed. (New York: Harper & Row, 1974).

8. Arthur Dyck, "Beneficent Euthanasia and Benemortasia," Kohl, op. cit., pp. 117-129.

12

Assisted Suicide
An Ethical Perspective

Gerald D. Coleman

. . . In its *Pastoral Constitution on the Church in the Modern World (Gaudium et Spes),* the Second Vatican Council taught that euthanasia is "opposed to life itself" and "violates the integrity of the human person."[1] This *Pastoral Constitution* teaches that whatever is opposed to life, such as euthanasia, is indeed an "infamy" and consequently a crime against humanity. This ethical affirmation has found subsequent repetition in important and pivotal documentation in the Roman Catholic Church.

In 1980, for example, the Congregation for the Doctrine of the Faith issued the *Declaration on Euthanasia.* This *Declaration* confirms and elaborates the teaching of the Second Vatican Council. It explains that human life is a gift from God over which humans have stewardship but not absolute dominion. Since life is the basis and necessary condition for all other human goods, its destruction is an especially grievous violation of the moral law, whether the victim consents or not.[2]

Particularly important is the *Declaration's* definition of euthanasia as "an action or an omission which of itself or by intention causes

Reprinted by permission of the publisher *Issues in Law and Medicine,* Vol. 3, No. 3, Winter 1987. Copyright © 1987 by the National Legal Center for the Medically Dependent & Disabled, Inc.

death, in order that all suffering may in this way be eliminated."[3] The *Declaration* thus affirms the teaching of Catholic theology that a deliberate effort to hasten someone's death is wrong whether achieved by gunshot or starvation. Morally what is important is that one intends the person's death, either as an end in itself, or as a means to another end, such as ending the person's suffering.

In 1984, the National Conference of Catholic Bishops of the United States of America issued *Guidelines for Legislation on Life-Sustaining Treatment*.[4] These *Guidelines* strongly assert that life is to be "celebrated" as a gift of the loving God and the life of every human person must be respected because all life is made in the image and likeness of God. These *Guidelines* support the "distinctive approach" of Catholic theology to the question of life and death as it emphasizes that the Catholic tradition not only condemns direct attacks on innocent life, but *also* promotes a general view of life as a sacred trust over which we can claim stewardship but not absolute dominion.[5]

> These *Guidelines* thus: Reaffirm public policies against homocide and assisted suicide. Medical treatment legislation may clarify procedures for discontinuing treatment which only secures a precarious and burdensome prolongation of life for the terminally ill patient, but should not condone or authorize any deliberate act or omission designed to cause a patient's death.[6]

Another example of this "distinctive approach" can be found in the front-page editorial of 25 January 1987 in *L'Osservatore Romano* entitled "With Regard to Euthanasia." This editorial was concerned with the Conference of Medical Associations of the European Community's recommendation of 15 January 1987 that "medicine needs in every circumstance to constantly·respect the life, moral autonomy, and free choice of the patient." The editorial criticizes the ambiguity of this statement for seemingly allowing a patient alone to judge what preserves human dignity. The editorial points out that physicians must always defend the exclusive dominion of God over human life and a sick person may never consent to terminate his or her life.

This same moral affirmation is found in the 1987 *Instruction on Respect for Human Life in Its Origin and on the Dignity of Procreation* of the Congregation for the Doctrine of the Faith.[7] this 1987 *Instruction* teaches:

> From the moment of conception, the life of every human being is
> to be respected in an absolute way because man is the only creature
> on earth that God has "wished for himself" and the spiritual soul
> of each man is "immediately created" by God; his whole being bears
> the image of the Creator. Human life is sacred because from its beginning
> it involves "the creative action of God" and it remains forever in a
> special relationship with the Creator, who is its sole end. God alone
> is the Lord of life from its beginning until its end: no one can, in
> any circumstance, claim for himself the right to destroy directly an
> innocent human being.[8]

In reading these documents, it is important to notice that the
net is cast widely in terms of the audience. This teaching about the
dignity of individual life appeals, as the *Declaration on Euthanasia*
points out, to Christians, other believers, and people of goodwill.
It is hoped, then, that the "distinctive approach" of Roman Catholic
teaching on the questions of life and death appeals to Christians in
that it speaks about the meaning of life and death from a Christological
perspective; to other believers it appeals to the dignity of the human
person; and to people of goodwill it appeals to human rights.

From a moral point of view, then, the teaching of the Roman
Catholic Church regarding human life sustains a clear "bias for life."
One would submit that this "bias for life" should inform all our
decisions in every critical matter regarding life and death. This "bias"
is *de facto* the foundation of the Judeo-Christian worldview as well
as the motivating force which undergirds medical research and practice.
It flows, for most people, from a theistic belief. However, as already
mentioned, it has been and can be affirmed by those whose views
of reality do not include the existence of God.

The "bias for life" requires that all individuals should direct their
efforts toward the sustaining of life where it exists.

. . . [T]hose who advocate the possibility of euthanasia generally
do so out of concern for those who, for whatever reason, face deep
and anguished suffering.

In light of this understandably human concern, it is critical to
realize that it *is* possible for persons to achieve goals that are encompassing, profound, and lasting and yet be in a state of great suffering.
It is essential to appreciate the fact that true human happiness cannot
be measured merely by pleasure, comfort, or freedom from anxiety,
tension, and guilt. Normally, pleasure, comfort, and peace are the

consequences and the signs of the achievement of authentic human goals and the fulfillment of the true human needs, and hence they are good and desirable, but they are secondary signs and not the proof or measure of real human achievement. In other words, we must not measure good and bad merely in terms of pleasure and pain.

The Christian faith looks upon suffering and death in two different ways. On the one hand, death is evil because it is the result of sin. On the other hand, it is a liberating and grace-filled experience, if the proper motivation is present. These two views are not contradictory; rather they are complimentary. Suffering and death, joined to the suffering and death of Jesus, represent not dissolution but growth, not punishment but fulfillment, not sadness but joy. God allows suffering and death to enable us to live with Christ now and forever. This principle, supremely exemplified in the Cross of Christ, is rooted in the basic human need to preserve life, since people suffer only in order to achieve a renewed, purified, and enriched life.[9]

It is important to appreciate, then, that suffering is not an absolute human evil. Although suffering is truly an ontological evil to be alleviated whenever possible, it is not of itself a moral evil nor without supernatural and human benefits. Some will certainly scoff at this view, but the Christian tradition holds that great good can come out of suffering when this is joined to the suffering of Jesus. This teaching does not imply a masochistic desire for pain, nor does it stand in the way of medical progress. Suffering, therefore, can be an authentic means of spiritual growth.

It is legitimate to conclude that a "speciality of the house" for all Christian churches should be to provide authentic healing whenever suffering is present. Suffering as a means of spiritual growth is not destroyed if pain-killing drugs are used to assist the suffering person. For example, the *Ethical and Religious Directives for Catholic Health Facilities* of the United States' Catholic Bishops teaches: "It is not euthanasia to give a dying person sedatives and analgesics for the alleviation of pain, when such measure is judged necessary, even though they may deprive the patient of the use of reason, or shorten his life."[10]

What is clear is that a patient is to be helped to complete his or her life with the maximum of peace and composure. Suffering, in other words, needs not be a wasteland but can be a vital time in one's life, a period of reconciling one's self to life and to death and for attaining interior peace.

Our suffering is *human* suffering; it has meaning and thus can be transcended. Suffering can be made redemptive through the sufferer's creative spirit. Pope John Paul II expresses this same vision: "Suffering has a special value in the eyes of the Church. It is something good, before which the Church bows down in reverence with all the depth of her faith in redemption."[11] Moreover, we make a sincere gift of self when we reach out to relieve suffering. As John Paul II affirms, "Christ has taught men to do good by His suffering and to do good to those who suffer. . . . No institution can by itself replace the human heart, human compassion, human love or human initiative, when it is a question of dealing with the sufferings of another."[12]

ETHICAL CONCLUSIONS

Although human suffering in its multiple dimensions is a factor of life which causes great pain and human anguish, it must not be used as a reason for justifying the direct taking of human life. From an ethical point of view, therefore, there is no justification for euthanasia, even when placed in the category of benemortasia. This conclusion is based on the principle integral to the Catholic moral tradition of the sanctity of all life, which concludes that every person's life must be reverenced because of its personal dignity and value. This "sanctity of life" principle is based on a variety of Christian doctrines, such as creation and redemption, the immortality of the soul, and a religious understanding of the human person. God must always be understood as the Creator and Sustainer of life. Norman St. John-Stevas situates this principle well: "The value of human life for the Christian in the first century A.D., as today, rested not on its development of the superior sentience but on the unique character of the union of a body and soul, both destined for eternal life. The right to life thus has a philosophical foundation. . . . Respect for the lives of *others* because of their eternal destiny is the essence of the Christian teaching."[13]

Paul Ramsey makes the important point that the sanctity of life is not a function of the worth any human person attributes to life, but that its primary value lies in the relation of life to God: "One grasps the religious outlook upon the sanctity of human life only if he sees that this life is asserted to be *surrounded* by sanctity that need not be in a man; that the most dignity a man ever possesses is a dignity that is alien to him. . . . A man's dignity is an overflow from God's dealing with him, and not primarily an anticipation of anything he will ever be by himself alone."[14] Therefore, life is always a guaranteed value or dignity because the only way life truly exists is in "covenant" or in relationship to God.

This grounding of the sanctity of life in religious convictions also has its equivalency in nonreligious groundings. The sociologist, Edward Shils, asks, "Is human life really sacred?" and responds, "I answer that it is, self-evidently. Its sacredness is the most primordial of experiences."[15] Shils thus contends: "The chief feature of the proto-religious, 'natural metaphysic' is the affirmation that life *is* sacred. It is believed to be sacred not because it is a manifestation of a transcendent Creator from whom life comes. . . . [Rather] the idea of sacredness is generated by the primordial experience of being alive, of experiencing the elemental sensation of vitality and the elemental fear of its extinction."[16]

What matters critically in the euthanasia discussion, therefore, is the acceptance or nonacceptance of the sanctity of life as a general principle. The sanctity of life principle must engender an attitude which fosters a strong bias in favor of human life and encourages us to act in ways consistent with this bias.

Central to both Catholic and Protestant theology on this question is the conviction that God is Lord of Life and Death. This conviction is another way of affirming that the ultimate value and sanctity of human life comes from God. This conviction implies that no one can ever claim total mastery over one's own or another's life. In other words, life is God's loan to us: not only because life is grounded in God, but also because God has given us life as a value to be held in trust and to be used according to his will. Saint Thomas Aquinas thus taught: "That a person has dominion over himself is because he is endowed with free choice. Thanks to that free choice a man is at liberty to dispose of himself with respect to those things in this life which are subject to his freedom. But the passage from this life to a happier one is not one of those things, for one's passage from this life is subject to the will and power of God."[17]

Human persons, then, have only a right to the use of human life, not to dominion over human life. What makes killing forbidden is that it usurps a divine prerogative and violates divine rights. When this conclusion is reached, moreover, the patient is never left alone. Advocacy of euthanasia does, in fact, leave the patient alone.[18] Every person is a locus of meaning and value. It matters, therefore, how a person dies. Those who advocate euthanasia or benemortasia actually allow a suffering person to die alone. Advocacy of assisted suicide is advocacy of defeat: a giving up on human life as sacred and filled with dignity.[19]

In his painting, "The Creation of Man," Marc Chagall paints at the bottom of the image an angel holding the limp body of Adam. At the top of the painting one finds some extraordinarily interesting symbols: the eight-branch candelabra of the Jewish faith, the scroll of the Law, the ladder, presumably Jacob's ladder, and the swirling sun from the story of Elijah in the Old Testament. On the other side of the sun, there appears certain symbols from the Christian faith: Jesus crucified, a fish, which is the symbol of the Eucharist, and the Tables of the Law. On the side there is a crowd of faces looking down on this whole event. Those faces look like a cheering crowd at a football game, presumably a crowd who are the children of Adam, all of us. The painting promises that, in a moment, the breath of God will enliven that limp figure, and it will come to life. And the first things that it will see are the cheering and smiling faces of all the children that will flow from this human being and all the symbols that our civilization has used to raise the great question of the meaning of life. The angel holding that body is true life support because that body will come to life, and know joy and know meaning and know sharing of fellowship in one's family and in one's culture.

Euthanasia and benemortasia are ethical postures which give up on "life support." Again and again, writers point out that it is not death itself but the dying process that frightens individuals. People want to make sure that they will not be sentenced to intractable pain and suffering. The appeal for release is certainly understandable, but killing the patient, even when done with the kindest of motives, is not the moral way to address the problem. There should be no passion for euthanasia or benemortasia.

NOTES

1. W. Abbott, *The Documents of Vatican II* (Piscataway, N.J.: New Century Publications, 1966), p. 226.

2. "Declaration on Euthanasia," in *Official Catholic Teachings: Update* 1980, p. 180.

3. Ibid., p. 183.

4. National Conference of Catholic Bishops, *Guidelines for Legislation on Life-Sustaining Treatment,* 1984, p. 526.

5. Ibid., pp. 526-527.

6. Ibid., p. 528.

7. J. Ratzinger, *Instruction on Respect for Human Life in Its Origin and on the Dignity of Procreation: Replies to Certain Questions of the Day* (Washington, D.C.: U.S. Catholic Conference, 1987).

8. Ibid., p. 5.

9. B. Ashley and K. O'Rourke, *Health Care Ethics: A Theological Perspective* (Washington, D.C.: Catholic Health Association, 1978).

10. *Ethical and Religious Directives for Catholic Health Facilities* (Washington, D.C.: Catholic Health Association, 1971), p. 7.

11. Pope John Paul, II, "On the Christian Meaning of Human Suffering," *L'Osservatore Romano* (February 20, 1984):1-8.

12. Ibid., p. 8, col. 1-2.

13. Norman St. John-Stevas, *The Right to Life* (1963), p. 12.

14. Paul Ramsey, "The Morality of Abortion," in *Life or Death: Ethics and Options,* edited by D. H. Laggy (1968), p. 71.

15. Edward Shils, "The Sanctity of Life," in *Life or Death: Ethics and Options,* edited by D. H. Laggy (1968), pp. 18-19

16. Ibid., p. 12.

17. Not every author agrees, of course, with this interpretation of "Dominion." For example, Richard Westley equates Creator and the creature more unequivocally than traditional authors. On the basis of an incarnational faith, Westley claims that the Divine and Human are so wedded to one another as to eliminate any talk of Divine and Human prerogatives. For Westley, the mystery of the incarnation tells us that God has chosen to make Divine work our own. Since God lives in us, whatever belongs to Divine Dominion also belongs to us. Westley thus challenges absolute sovereignty and limited stewardship by exploring the meaning of life as a "gift" from God. As Westley sees it, if life is given as a gift, then it is subject to our freedom and to speak of stewardship is out of place in this context. See R. Westley, *Morality and Its Beyond* (Mystic, Conn.: Twenty-Third Publications, 1984).

18. Joseph Fletcher, "The 'Right' to Life and the 'Right' to Die," in *Beneficent Euthanasia* (Buffalo, N.Y.: Prometheus Books, 1975), pp. 44-53.

19. Richard Gula, *What Are They Saying about Euthanasia?* (Mahwah, N.J.: Paulist Press, 1986).

13

Assisting Suicide
An Ethical Perspective

Ernlé W. D. Young

Although the primary intent of this [chapter] is to provide an ethical perspective on assisting *those who are terminally ill* to end their own lives, it will be helpful to begin the analysis by reflecting on suicide in general.

One of the advantages of a principled approach to ethics, whether deontological or rule utilitarian,[1] is that one does not have to reinvent the wheel each time one confronts a moral dilemma or faces a moral decision. Principles, serving as guiding norms, express the distillation of human moral wisdom. They suggest what, *prima facie,* one ought or ought not to do in a given situation. What one actually does, or does not do, or which among competing principles one chooses to protect, will, of course, depend on the facts of the case and, at least if one subscribes to the theory of W. D. Ross, a consequentialist calculation about which principle, above all others, will serve to maximize utility.[2]

With respect to the issue of suicide, in general, two moral principles are always potentially in conflict. On the one hand, there is the principle

Reprinted by permission of the publisher *Issues in Law & Medicine* Vol. 3, No. 3, Winter 1987. Copyright © 1987 by the National Legal Center for the Medically Dependent & Disabled, Inc.

of autonomy, from the Greek words *autos* (self) and *nomos* (law). This principle holds that, so far as is possible and consistent with the welfare of others, persons ought to be respected as and encouraged to be self-determining moral agents. Immanuel Kant (a rule deontologist) argued in his *Groundwork of the Metaphysic of Morals* that persons should always be treated as autonomous ends and never merely as means to the ends of others.[3] John Stuart Mill (one of the fathers of rule-utilitarianism) speaks of the individuality of action and thought in his celebrated treatise, *On Liberty*.[4] What Mill means by individuality is similar to what Kant denotes by the term autonomy. In our time, the consumer movement has stressed the importance of the autonomy of the consumer (whether of medical services or of other goods).[5] From the perspective of the principle of autonomy, the wish of someone to choose death rather than life ought to be respected, *providing that sound evidence shows that the person concerned is mentally competent and rational* (and that, therefore, the decision is in fact substantially autonomous). In the case of the mentally competent and rational person, suicide may be regarded as the ultimate expression of autonomy. Such an individual expresses the will to be self-determining, not only in matters of life, but also in the manner and timing of death. So long as acting on the basis of this principle does not harm others, it would be consistent with Mill's individuality of action and thought.

On the other hand, there is the principle of beneficence. Beneficence imposes on us a duty to benefit others, when in a position to do so. This principle is deeply embedded in the history of medicine and the medical ethical tradition. The Hippocratic corpus enjoins the physician not only to avoid inflicting harm on patients, but positively to benefit them.[6] Beneficence readily lends itself to paternalistic behavior. In the ethical literature, paternalism refers "to practices that restrict the liberty of individuals, without their consent, where the justification for such actions is either the prevention of some harm they will do to themselves or the production of some benefit for them they would not otherwise secure."[7]

In the normal course of events, it would be almost instinctive for the physician to act paternalistically and beneficently to attempt to save the life of someone who had tried to kill herself. In so deciding, the physician would be making the assumption that the suicidal person was not, at the time, mentally competent and rational. This, in turn, reflects a value judgment: no one "in his right mind" would want to kill himself;

to want to kill oneself, one must be, in this conception, mentally off-balance or emotionally unhinged—at least temporarily. That the majority within our society subscribe to this value judgment sanctions the automatic paternalistic application of the principle of beneficence. For example, whenever someone is brought into an emergency room as the result of an overdose of some type of medication, such a person is presumed to have been mentally incompetent and irrational at the time the overdose was taken. The principle of beneficence, paternalistically applied (as is bound to be the case in an emergent situation), therefore requires that the stomach be pumped out, that the drug used be identified, and that immediate measures be taken to counter the effects of the drug—including, if necessary, cardiopulmonary resuscitation, ventilatory support, renal dialysis, and other intensive care interventions.

The principle of autonomy, therefore, is constantly in tension with the principle of beneficence. The wish to respect other people as self-determining moral agents (so long as their actions are not infringing upon the liberties of others or causing others harm, and so long as they are mentally competent and rational) is inherently opposed to the duty, negatively, to prevent harm from coming to them, or, positively, to benefit them. Death is valued negatively in our culture (with some few exceptions, presently to be considered); life is valued positively. Averting harm, then, is equated with preventing someone else from dying, and benefiting another is synonomous with intervening to enable that person to live.

In the absence of an underlying terminal and painful disease process, the principle of beneficence ought *prima facie* to take precedence over the principle of autonomy in responding to suicidal attempts or desires. When the suicidal person does have an underlying terminal and painful medical condition, or is in an advanced state of decrepitude, and is mentally competent and rational, however, the principle of autonomy ought *prima facie* to be ranked in priority over the principle of beneficence.

The first position hinges on the value judgment, shared by most people in our society, that, in the absence of some major misfortune, medical or otherwise, and on balance, life is preferable to death. Obviously, this is a value judgment not endorsed by everybody. Of serious concern to many of us are the data, beginning to be accumulated, which indicate the alienation of significant numbers of young people from this shared value.[8]

Two verses from a poem written a year ago by a seventeen-year-old boy from an affluent home exemplify this alienation:

> Inside my head is pounding
> Been hurting me for weeks
> I've got to find salvation
> I've got to find some peace.
>
> I just now realized
> I have new decisions to make
> What building shall I jump from
> What pills should I take?

Despite being scholarly, athletic, musical, handsome, and in other ways gifted, Todd, a year after writing these lines, leaped to his death from a high-rise building on the campus where he was a student. He was one of the approximately six thousand who succeeded in killing themselves out of the estimated four hundred thousand young people who attempt suicide each year.[9] The recent spate of group teenage suicides and attempted suicides indicates how profoundly foreign to many of our young people are the values of their elders on the issue of suicide.

Values and value judgments, which enter decisively into the ethical decisions we make, whether consciously or unconsciously, are correlated closely with deeply-held metaphysical beliefs. Those who, standing within the Judeo-Christian tradition, affirm life (with all its problems and difficulties) to be a good gift from the hand of God, will be prone to value life above death, even in the worst of times. Those who, less directly connected to any religious tradition, nevertheless, affirm an evolutionary and optimistic worldview (e.g., the American dream), will also tend, on the whole and except under extreme stress, to value life above death. In both instances, value judgments are being made. The young, standing in the shadow of nuclear proliferation and annihilation, are understandably less easily able to believe that good will always and automatically triumph over evil, that the light will invariably drive back the darkness. With the belief and value systems of previous generations no longer credible to them, it should not surprise us that a disturbingly high number of young people will not automatically value life above death—even in the absence of profound personal affliction.

Nevertheless, those who, on balance, value life more than death constitute a majority within society. This majority, therefore, would endorse the primacy of beneficence over autonomy when someone is threatening or attempting to commit suicide—so long as there is no known underlying terminal disease process, increasing physical decrepitude, or unmitigable pain. The presumption (on the basis of the value judgment) is that this person's autonomy had been compromised (either by extrinsic or intrinsic factors) and that the threatened or attempted suicide was therefore not a truly autonomous act. The intention of intervening would be not only to prevent the death of the suicidal person but also to provide him with such appropriate therapy, counseling, or support as would serve eventually to remove the impediments to substantial autonomy that prevent him from affirming the goodness of life. A further assumption is that, if the intervention is effective (in both senses), the suicidal person would later provide *retrospective consent* to what was done to prevent death and to remove the obstacles to autonomy. It is anticipated that looking back, once the crisis is passed, the person who was previously suicidal will be glad and grateful that action was taken, on the basis of paternalistic beneficence, to avert death. That there is often empirical evidence, *ex post facto,* to indicate that these presumptions were, in fact, correct, further strengthens the bias in favor of subordinating autonomy to beneficence in the circumstance we are discussing.[10]

However, a majority in our society is also beginning to recognize that, when a person is afflicted with an underlying terminal condition, or is in a state of advanced physical decrepitude, or is in unmitigable pain, a distinction must be drawn between *extending life* (with all that makes life rich and full) and *merely prolonging an inevitable process of dying.* On the basis of this distinction, there may be a point beyond which life is no longer necessarily to be valued above death. In fact, the opposite may be the case—especially when the person is experiencing pain that cannot be alleviated. Now, *prima facie,* the principle of autonomy may in good conscience be ranked above the principle of beneficence—so long as the person concerned is mentally competent and rational, and so long as all possible steps have been taken to minimize the ensuing harm to others.[11]

This leads to the following conclusion: if (a) a person is either terminally ill or irreversibly decrepit in terms of physical functioning; (b) and is in unmitigable pain—whether physical or psychological, or both; (c) and is obviously mentally competent and rational; and (d) has attempted to mitigate the harmful effects—especially predictable feelings of guilt—of her action on those who will survive her, then it is morally licit to rank the principle of autonomy above the principle of beneficence in evaluating one's duty to respond to that person's suicidal attempts or desires. This means that the suicidal intent may now be perceived simply as the final expression of autonomy, deserving to be respected as such without any attempt to prevent it by paternalistically beneficent intervention.

However, at this juncture, a theological caveat may be in order. From a theological perspective, suicide may be regarded as a predictable response to the breakdown of *faith* (the ability to affirm the essential meaningfulness of human existence, especially in the face of pain), *hope* (being able to look at the future with confidence and courage, especially in circumstances of present distress), and *love* (the ability to affirm the self and to receive from and give to others a similar affirmation). When terminal illness and the pain associated with it are experienced as essentially *meaningless,* when the future is perceived as holding nothing but further affliction and debilitation and there *no longer appear to be grounds for confidence and courage with respect to what is yet to be,* and when it seems that significant others *no longer care nor want to be cared for,* then the wish to choose death above life is eminently reasonable and understandable. "Why does anyone commit suicide?" ask Kastenbaum and Aisenberg.[12] Their response focuses merely on the first of the three theological ingredients we have identified (which they deem sufficient): "[M]ost generally, because life has no meaning."[13]

Nevertheless, before simply giving "permission" to someone who is terminally ill and in intractable pain to translate the suicidal desire into the deed, it is first of all necessary, from a theological perspective, for the caregiver to attempt to help that person discover or recover faith, hope, and love. In other words, one's primary obligation, theologically understood, is to endeavor to enable the terminally ill and suicidal person to find or regain a sense of the meaningfulness of all human experience—pain included. It is to attempt to facilitate in that person the capacity to look into the future with confidence and courage, especially if his vision can be extended beyond the horizons of time to the limitless vistas of eternity. And it is to try to instill in him the conviction that he is essentially lovable—no matter how his outward appearance may be changing, even deteriorating, from day to day, making it more and more difficult for him to love himself—and, therefore, capable of loving and being loved.

Such an attempt may or may not involve the use of religious figures and religious language. Spirituality is a category of human experience broader and more universal than religion, yet including it. It is possible to speak of faith, hope, and love in either religious or secular language. Whether religious or secular symbols are employed will depend on the belief and value system of the suicidal person—again, because of the principle of autonomy. To attempt to impose one's own particular religious beliefs or values on others—for whatever good intentions—betrays a lack of respect for their autonomy and may even violate it.

Only after the attempt has been made, seriously and strenuously, to enable the dying person to find or regain faith, hope, and love, and has failed, is it morally permissible to acquiesce in her wish to choose death rather than life. Only then is it morally licit to allow her to express her autonomy in this ultimate way rather than intervening with beneficently paternalistic motivation to frustrate it.

However, it is one thing to acquiesce; it is another to assist. Acquiescing in a terminally ill person's desire to end his life may be morally appropriate, especially where the conditions outlined above have been satisfied. Can the same be said of assisting? This is the issue to be taken up.

The first question to be raised is: Is there a moral difference between someone saying to someone who wishes to commit suicide, "I'll not stop you" and "I'll help you"? In saying "I'll not stop you," one may be expressing respect for a state of mind, a belief system, or an intention to act in a certain way, which may, in the circumstances, seem to be appropriate for the person concerned. For one to say "I'll help you," on the other hand, would require a much higher level of personal assent to the state of mind, the belief system, or the intention to act being evidenced. There is a difference between respect and assent. One may respect the views of Jehovah's Witnesses and of Marxists, but not assent to them. One may or may not assent to the suicidal desire being expressed which, for reasons already given, one may respect. If one cannot assent to the suicidal ideation, even though one may respect it, there is no moral obligation to go beyond saying, "I'll not stop you," to "I'll help you." If one can assent to the suicidal wish, and all the reasons for it that the person concerned might adduce, then, as expressive of his own autonomy, one may choose to say, "I'll help you."

The crucial point is that were one to say, "I'll help you," one would be acting autonomously and out of generosity, not because of a perceived moral obligation or duty. One of the principal reasons for choosing to help a suicidal person in the circumstances we are considering is compassion. However, acting on the basis of the principle of beneficence would require of the person assisting a stronger conviction that, in this particular situation, death would actually be a benefit, than acting on the basis of the principle of autonomy. It also presumes that there is a "right" to help which carries with it a concomitant duty. Beneficence requires help as a duty; autonomy allows assistance as a freely offered gift. There is no duty to help someone who wishes to die to accomplish her death, since there is no corresponding "right" to be helped to die. However, assistance may freely be proffered as an act of generosity and compassion— in circumstances where one not only respects, but also assents to, the suicidal intention being expressed.

There are various factors which may lead one to go on to assent to views which, on other grounds, one might already respect. One would be the quality of the relationship with the person who now wishes to end her life. Another would be the degree to which one shares that person's values, belief systems, and reasoned arguments for wanting to end his life. Yet another would be the inability of the person wishing to die to accomplish his own death without assistance. A fourth would be the capacity of the person being asked for assistance to provide it. Where the relationship between potential helper and helpee is extremely close, where there is a high degree of assent to the values, beliefs, and arguments being expressed by the person contemplating suicide, where the person rationally wanting to die cannot possibly accomplish this without assistance (the case of the person with end-stage multiple sclerosis comes to mind), and where there are ways in which the potential helper can in fact help, then, while there may be no *duty* to assist, it would be difficult to argue that it would be *immoral* autonomously to choose to help.

Tristram Englehardt goes further. He argues in support of the right of individuals to commit suicide, and then concludes: "Insofar as individuals possess this right for themselves, they should have as well the right to be aided by others."[14] This seems to me not necessarily to follow and to go too far. The language of "rights" in this context implies corresponding duties. There is no duty to help someone to die, although, as has already been stated, one may voluntarily choose to provide assistance as a freely offered act of kindness.

The motivation of the potential helper is crucial. Where the motive for offering help is indeed to benefit the person wishing to die, this is morally acceptable. But where the motive is selfish, as in an attempt to inherit the estate of the person wishing to die, this obviously would cast an altogether different light on the assistance being contemplated. Because motivation cannot be assessed before the fact, helping another person to die should never be given legal sanction.

This brings us to the final issue: the nature of the assistance that might be given, were one to be morally convinced of the appropriateness of helping someone who, on grounds discussed above, wanted to commit suicide but was unable to accomplish this act. Various possible types of assistance come to mind, ranging from seemingly innocent to far more incriminating. The options would include:

(a) Encouragement. Removing obstacles in the way of the person wishing to end their life, for example, by reassuring them that they will not be judged and damned by God; or suggesting that, if the roles were reversed, one would probably be contemplating suicide oneself.

(b) Information, of the sort provided by the "Hemlock Society" or "Exit"[15] about how to accomplish one's own death in the least traumatic and most effective manner.

(c) Provisions or procurement of the necessary means when the suicidal person is and would otherwise be without such means.

(d) Helping to administer the means to be employed, e.g., mixing the lethal dose and holding it to the lips of the person wishing to die, or holding the gun to the suicidal person's head and placing his finger on the trigger.

(e) Actually killing the person wishing to die, at their request, for example, by smothering, shooting, or poisoning. The line between assisted suicide of this kind and voluntary "mercy killing" is blurred. It is difficult to discern a moral difference between them.

As was suggested earlier, the spectrum of possibilities, outlined above, includes relatively innocuous forms of assistance, at the one end, and, at the other, the serious matter of taking the life of another human being. Each option might be considered moral, so long as the person wishing to die meets the criteria previously discussed, and so long as the motivation of the person providing assistance is solely that of wanting to benefit the dying person. How far along the spectrum, the helper will be willing to go, will depend on the factors previously mentioned: the quality of the relationship; the degree to which the beliefs, values, and arguments for wanting to die of the person seeking help are persuasive to the person in a position to help; the degree of inability of the suicidal person to accomplish the desired death; and the capacity—emotionally as well as practical—of the person being asked for help to provide it.

What is obvious is that the consequences of helping become much more serious as one moves from (a) through (e). Providing the sorts of assistance suggested in (d) and (e) could result in the helper being required to face civil or criminal charges. However, the helper who deeply loves the person wishing to die, shares his beliefs and values and is persuaded by his reasons for wanting to die, and is in a position to help—both emotionally and practically—may be willing to risk the adverse consequences and go as far as (d) or (e) where the person wishing to die is entirely incapable of accomplishing his own death. Were one so to act, this would be an act of compassion and courage of the highest order.

In conclusion, some legal implications must be drawn out from the argument that has been made, with a few recommendations to follow. We have outlined a range of possible responses to people who, for whatever reason, no longer regard life as a benefit and choose, rationally and competently, to act autonomously and commit suicide. In the case of those not afflicted with an underlying terminal illness, nor in a state of advanced decrepitude, the *prima facie* presumption is that their competency is in some way impaired or compromised and that, therefore, the principle of beneficence ought to take priority over the principle of autonomy. If, later, it is established that, with full rationality and competency, death was still being valued above life, and every possible effort has been made to enable the suicidal person to view life differently, as a benefit rather than a detriment, and had failed, then, reluctantly, on the basis of the principle of autonomy, one would be required to acquiesce in the decision to die. It follows, *ipso facto,* that, if such suicidal attempts were unsuccessful, the persons concerned should not be subject to criminal charges.

Even more insistently, one must object to criminal charges being brought against those who unsuccessfully had tried to end their own lives in circumstances of terminal illness or advanced decrepitude and unmitigable pain, where every effort had been made to minimize for the survivors the untoward consequences of the act.

The more difficult question is what legal consequences, if any, ought to be borne by those who assist people in the above category. For the reasons set out below, my own convictions are that encouragement or the provision of information ought not to be subject to legal penalties, that helping someone to accomplish his own death or actually to kill him (at his request) ought to be subject to legal penalties of a special lesser kind, and that procuring for someone who wishes to die the means necessary to accomplish it falls into an ambiguous category.

Encouraging or providing information to someone who wishes to die, in the circumstances we have asserted to be morally licit, represents a fairly modest step from acquiescence to assent and is consistent with it. Both are forms of assistance which affirm the autonomy of the person wishing to die. It would be hypocritical to argue that, while autonomy ought to be respected, acts which affirm or enhance autonomy ought to be subject to criminal charges. However, directly to assist the person to die or actually to kill her, even at her own request, are far more serious actions, susceptible to more serious kinds of abuse (for example, by those whose motivation is self interest rather than altruism). Because it is usually possible to be certain about motivation only *after-the-fact,* such actions should be subject to close legal scrutiny. This would require civil or criminal charges being brought against those so assisting or killing. However, in those cases where the motivation was demonstrably altruistic, the *penalties* ought to be light or nonexistent. To subject persons found guilty of killing for reasons of compassion to the same penalties as those found guilty of first- or second-degree murder seems excessive, unjust, and unwarranted.

This leaves the "ambiguous" category of those who procure for someone who wishes to end their own life, in the circumstances we are describing, the means that one is unable to obtain for oneself. Here, it seems that the "criminality," if any, of the assistance given should depend on a case by case assessment of what help was actually afforded. A physician who appropriately prescribes sleeping pills for a terminally ill patient ought not to be subject to criminal charges should the patient swallow all the pills at once, rather than two at a time, in order to end their life. On the other hand, a physician who inappropriately prescribes a medication whose sole effect is to cause death ought to be subject to civil or criminal charges. Again, should the motivation subsequently be proven to be compassion, the penalties should be light or nonexistent. Unless legal penalties are possible, even in cases where it was appropriate to help someone to die, the door could easily be opened to the inappropriate shortening of other's lives.

This leads to this [chapter's] final recommendations. Any remaining laws treating suicide as a criminal offense ought to be struck down. Laws forbidding the provision of assistance to someone wishing to die ought to be struck down, where the assistance is merely that of offering encouragement or providing information. And laws forbidding the provision of other kinds of assistance to someone wanting to die as in (c), (d), and (e), above ought to remain in place, but the penalties ought to be light or nonexistent in cases where it is clearly established that the motivation of the helper was not at all sinister, but unambiguously reflected compassion and altruism.[16]

NOTES

1. The word "deontological" derives from the Greek word *deon*, which means "duty" or "it is required." A deontological approach to ethics insists that, *a priori*, certain things are required of us, e.g., being truthful, and keeping promises. Conversely, a "rule-utilitarian" ethic is a system in which the "principle of utility" (deference to what will promote maximal general good, see, e.g., Mill, "Utilitarianism," in *Utilitarianism, Liberty, and Representative Government, Selections from August Comte and Positivism* [H. B. Acton ed. 1972]) is used to determine the rules that will be used to guide proper conduct. See generally Beauchamp and Childress, *Principles of Biomedical Ethics* ch. 2 (2d ed. 1983) which also constitutes a good example of the combination of two approaches. Ibid., p. x, chs. 3-6.

2. Whereas, in rule-utilitarianism, the principle of utility is employed

to fashion the rules themselves as well as to apply them. See Beauchamp and Childress, *supra* note 1, pp. 25-26, 30-32. W. D. Ross uses a consequentialist calculus to determine which deontological principle to apply in a particular situation where different principles compete for primacy. W. D. Ross, *Foundations of Ethics* (1939), pp. 175-191 .

3. I. Kant, *Groundwork of the Metaphysic of Morals* (trans. H. J. Paton 1964), pp. 95-96.

4. J. S. Mill, *On Liberty* (introd. R. Kirk 1955), but see especially ch. 3.

5. In the 1970s, a host of books was published encouraging medical consumer assertiveness on the basis of the principle of autonomy. See, e.g., A. S. Freese, *Managing Your Doctor: How to Get the Best Possible Care* (1975); G. J. Annas, *The Right of Hospital Patients: The Basic Civil Liberties Guide to a Hospital Patient's Rights* (1975); A. Levin, *Talk Back to Your Doctor: How to Demand (and Recognize) High Quality Health Care* (1975); S. E. Sagov and A. Brodsky, *The Active Patient's Guide to Better Medical Care* (1976); The Boston Women's Health Book Collective, *Our Bodies, Ourselves* (1976). It is also interesting to note that "The Patient's Bill of Rights," 42, C.F.R. §§405.1121, 442.311, assumed currency during the seventies.

6. For a fuller discussion of the principles of autonomy and beneficence, see Beauchamp and Childress, *supra* note 1, ch. 3 and 5, respectively, and also I. Englehardt, *The Foundations of Bioethics* (1986), pp. 66-87.

7. Beauchamp, "Paternalism," in *Encyclopedia of Bioethics* (W. T. Reich ed. 1978), pp. 1194-1201.

8. The 1980 edition of the *Statistical Abstract of the United States* reveals that suicide ranks among the top five causes of death for white males aged 10-55, and is the *second-ranked cause of death for all males aged 15-24.* Nearly 30,000 Americans a year choose to end their own lives; many experts believe that the official statistics grossly understate the actual number of suicides, perhaps by half.

9. 1984 figures.

10. "Generally, persons who use the most-lethal methods in their suicide attempts and are unsuccessful have a lower risk of future suicide attempts than do those who use the less-lethal methods. In other words, the person who survives a self-inflicted gunshot wound is less likely to try suicide again than someone who unsuccessfully used a plastic bag." L. A. de Spelder and A. L. Strickland, *The Last Dance: Encountering Death and Dying* (1983), p. 364.

11. It is only recently that a concerted effort has been made to substantiate the negative psychological, sociological, and physical effects of suicide on survivors. See Welu, "Pathological Bereavement: A Plan for Its Prevention," in *Bereavement: Its Psychosocial Aspects* (B. Schoenberg ed. 1975), 139.

12. R. Kastenbaum and R. Aisenberg, *The Psychology of Death* (1972), p. 251.

13. Ibid.

14. Englehardt, *supra* note 6, p. 306.

15. The Hemlock Society was founded in 1980. It supports the options of active voluntary euthanasia for the terminally ill and assisted suicide. See D. Humphrey, *Let Me Die Before I Wake* (3d ed. 1984). "Exit" is the British equivalent of the Hemlock Society.

16. From a tangled history in which it was often deemed a crime against the sovereign or state, and a sin against God—with the victim's body buried ignominiously or his estate forfeited to the crown as punishment—suicide in American law is expressly regarded a crime now in only two states: Alabama and South Carolina. Several jurisprudential considerations seem to have propelled the decriminalization here: the futility of branding criminal an act which, by its very definition, permanently places the perpetrator beyond the chastening grasp of the state, the unfairness of punishing a suicide victim's survivors by disseising them of the suicide's estate, and the pointlessness, if not the unconscionability, of risking further brutalization of the suicide victim's survivors by subjecting his corpse to ignominy.

It is thus accurate to say, as matters of both legal and actual fact, that suicide is not punished criminally anywhere in the United States. Moral revulsion toward suicide, and convictions that on some level it is tragic—however unpreventable actually or unpunishable legally—survive in the form of strong judicial and legislative condemnations of the act. Attempted suicide is also not punished criminally anywhere in the United States, preference being given to the view that people who try to kill themselves need medical help, not chastisement.

On the other hand, helping someone commit suicide is, by and large, still a crime in nearly every state in the nation. A large number of states has even passed legislation expressly criminalizing the act of aiding or abetting suicide. Yet even in the absence of such statutes, some courts have held guilty of murder persons who aid in suicide by providing the means of death.

For general background on, as well as specific state-by-state analysis of, laws regarding suicide, attempted suicide and assisting suicide, see Marzen, O'Down, Crone and Balch, "Suicide: A Constitutional Right?" 24 *Duquesne Law Review* 1 (1985):17-100, 148-242.

14

Justifiable Active Euthanasia in the Netherlands

Pieter Admiraal

Justifiable active euthanasia is practiced in Holland only with patients who are in the terminal phase of an incurable, usually malignant, disease. We offer these patients the best possible terminal care and euthanasia may be the last dignified act.

Euthanasia is widely accepted in Holland and up to five thousand cases are performed annually; but it is still illegal and every doctor who practices it is liable to prosecution. However, such prosecutions are not pursued provided that certain clearly circumscribed guidelines are followed; the law then accepts that the doctor acted under a conflict of duties in which he submitted to the force majeure, the merciful moral compulsion to relieve the patient of unbearable suffering.

Under these guidelines, the patient must have been informed of his situation and must have requested euthanasia freely as the result of careful consideration; the doctor must believe that termination of the patient's life was justified because there were no alternatives to the patient's untenable situation; the doctor had to have consulted another, independent doctor and filed a report about the case. After performing euthanasia, a doctor must report an unnatural death to

From *Free Inquiry* 9, No. 1 (Winter 1988-89). Reprinted by permission of the publisher.

the coroner; the police will investigate the case and report to the prosecutor, who, in consultation with the Attorney General, will decide whether to prosecute.

Very rarely does a patient in the early stages of disease decide to refuse treatment or want to die. Normally, patients want to live, want to fight their disease, want to accept all and any kind of treatment available even if it is only palliative and has terrible side effects; most patients hope to be cured even after the doctor has told them they have lost the fight. Often they want to go on and will try alternative medicine. The will to live, to survive, is one of the most basic human desires. What, then, makes a patient request euthanasia?

A patient will request euthanasia only after long consideration and only when his suffering becomes unbearable. And what constitutes unbearable suffering? There are closely related physical and psychological causes.

The physical causes include:

1. Loss of strength, especially in cachectic patients, sometimes so severe that the patient becomes totally incapable of any physical exertion.

2. Fatigue, even without physical effort, experienced as exhaustion.

3. Shortness of breath as a result of lung aberrations or tumors in the trachea or mouth cavity. Serious stridor or even suffocation may result.

4. Nausea and vomiting as the result of blockage of the esophagus or gastrointestinal tract or as the side effect of analgesics of cytotoxics.

5. Incontinence.

6. Sleeplessness, especially in patients with pain, fatigue, and apnea.

7. Pain. I will discuss this point in detail, because in all literature about dying, suffering, and euthanasia, pain is mentioned as the most important cause of physical and psychological suffering.

The majority of cancer patients will be in pain as a result of the tumor or its metastases. The intensity may vary from mild to agonizing. Patients and even doctors identify cancer with pain and speak about "cancer pain," which is said to be worse than normal pain. So there are many reasons to fear such a pain.

In fact, for most patients "cancer pain" means real physical pain combined with fear, sorrow, depression, and exhaustion. This kind of "pain" is an alarm signal indicating shortcomings in interhuman contact and misunderstandings of the patient's situation. One can treat this "pain" with good terminal care based on warm human contact.

Physical pain can be adequately controlled in most cases with morphine-like analgesics and/or psychopharmaceuticals, which block sensitive or sympathetic nervous tissue without adversely affecting the normal psychological functions of the patient. Thus physical pain alone as a reason for euthanasia is not usually medically justified.

Psychological causes include:

1. Psychic suffering as a result of the above-mentioned somatic problems.

2. Anxieties about pain and suffering, about spiritual and physical deformation, about becoming completely dependent and needing total nursing care, and about dying itself.

3. Grief about the loss of family and possessions; sorrow when grief is bottled up and not understood by others; bitter grief when the patient asks why this happens to him at this point in life. Grief can turn into rancor, revolt, aggression, and depression.

These problems lead to physical and psychological exhaustion despite all medical, nursing, and spiritual care. Incontinence, decubitis, fatigue, and loss of strength are considered by the patient to be especially degrading and undeserved and are perceived as symptoms of the complete loss of human dignity. This total disintegration of humanness causes unbearable suffering. Thus, as I said earlier, euthanasia in our hospitals is a dignified last act of assistance to a patient in his terminal phase. We use a combination of barbiturate and curare, according to the Manual of the Royal Society of Pharmacy; the death is painless.

Active euthanasia requires a long decision-making process that involves the patient, his next-of-kin, the doctor and other medical personnel, and often the patient's pastor or priest. The possibility of euthanasia is discussed with the patients in our hospital long before they enter the terminal phase of their diseases. Patients in the Netherlands know that they may ask for euthanasia the moment they judge their suffering to be unbearable; but they also know very well that the terminal care team has to make the decision of whether or not to carry out this request. Usually the patient's first request provides extra stimulus for the team to try to improve medical and spiritual care. We don't like to perform euthanasia and never suggest it to a patient.

The moment that all members of the medical team agree that there is no way to lessen the patient's suffering, that his suffering is unbearable, and that the guidelines have been fulfilled, the decision for active euthanasia is made. This decision and the reasoning behind it are frankly discussed with everyone involved, including the patient, before the act is performed. The day the euthanasia is carried out, the family is present in most cases. The pastor may be there on the request of the patient, and two nurses are also present. Though it is obviously a sad occasion, most people are filled with the relief that comes from knowing that they helped to end the suffering of a loved one in his final days.

REFERENCES

Admiraal, P. V., "Euthanasia Applied at a General Hospital," *The Euthanasia Review* 1 (1986):97.
———, "Justifiable Euthanasia," *Issues in Law & Medicine* 3 (1988):361.

15

Active Voluntary Euthanasia
A Needless Pandora's Box

D. Alan Shewmon

. . . One of the main reasons why the legal and medical professions have always opposed active euthanasia is that such societal issues are never static; they necessarily evolve according the the dynamics of their underlying philosophy, with the laws being forever revised to accommodate it. Because the logical endpoint of that evolution is considered undesirable, so is its initiation.

Euthanasia advocates dismiss the "slippery slope" argument by reference to other societies in which the practice of suicide for specific indications has not evolved into a horror of abuses—for example, the voluntary freezing to death of elderly Eskimos.[1] But such societies are not valid testing grounds for voluntary euthanasia in our own society, because of the differences in basic philosophy and the radically different levels of social complexity. The Netherlands would serve this purpose well, except for the fact that insufficient time has passed, since acceptance of active euthanasia, to observe any long-term effects. Our similarities with pre-Nazi Germany, however, are compelling, and will be discussed later. Thus, the President's Commission stated:

Reprinted by permission of the publisher *Issues in Law & Medicine* Vol. 3, No. 3, Winter 1987. Copyright © 1987 by the National Legal Center for the Medically Dependent & Disabled, Inc.

"Obviously, slippery slope arguments must be very carefully employed less they serve merely as an unthinking defense of the status quo. . . . Nevertheless, the Commission has found that in [this] area . . . valid concerns warrant being especially cautious before adopting any policy that weakens the protections against taking human life."[2]

In what follows, it will be shown that this particular "slippery slope" is not merely a theoretical possibility; it is a present reality. The practice of euthanasia will necessarily facilitate this ongoing evolution along at least two[3] dimensions simultaneously: the scope of indications (beginning with terminal illness and ending with euthanasia "on demand") and the degree of voluntariness (beginning with voluntary euthanasia and ending with involuntary "euthanasia" for the benefit of others).

FIRST DIMENSION: FROM TERMINAL ILLNESS TO EUTHANASIA ON DEMAND

The Inherent Ambiguity of "Terminal Illness"

According to the *Hemlock Manifesto,* formulated in 1982, one of the guiding principles for the practice of active voluntary euthanasia ought to be that the recipient have a "terminal illness," meaning that "the person is likely, in the judgment of two examining physicians, to die of that condition within six months."[4] But prognoses for survival are never that accurate; about 10 percent of patients admitted to hospices to die end up being discharged home because of either remission or inappropriate diagnosis.[5]

The Inherent Unenforceability of the Proposed Criteria

Moreover, the six month cut-off is arbitrary. Proponents argue that arbitrary line-drawing is unavoidable in many areas that are nonetheless beneficial (e.g., highway speed limits), but statutory arbitrariness in this area will certainly encourage judicial discretion far beyond the literal interpretation of any such requirement. If one receives a speeding ticket and defends oneself in court on the basis that speed limits are inherently arbitrary, one will most likely wind up paying the fine. But if a doctor were to administer euthanasia to someone projected to die within seven months who kept pleading for "deliverance," it is not likely that he would be charged with murder, or even for aiding and abetting suicide, if active euthanasia at six months were recognized not only as legal but as good. This is especially true given that the present cut-off of zero months is already not enforced (most defendants in mercy killings or assisted suicides are acquitted).[6] Regardless of where the time limit is placed, there will be patients just beyond it who will demand their "right" to euthanasia; then the advocacy groups will seek to abolish the manifest hypocrisy of the already liberalized law. Once set in motion, this positive feedback cannot halt until its logical culmination in euthanasia on demand.

Expanding Criteria within the Euthanasia Movement Itself

The reality of this slippery slope is evident within the euthanasia movement itself. Much of what follows pertains to the Hemlock Society as a specific example, only because, of all the "right-to-die" societies, it is the most forthright about its goal to promote active euthanasia. It began as an advocate of active voluntary euthanasia for the terminally ill. Hemlock's *Manifesto* declares that "[i]ncurable distress is a legally insufficient basis for justification [of euthanasia] unless it is a product of terminal illness."[7]

Nevertheless, with the passage of time, Hemlock began to refer to itself as "a society supporting the option of voluntary euthanasia . . . for the terminally ill, or the seriously incurably physically ill."[8] Nowhere in any of their literature is the concept "incurably physically ill" defined, but it is obviously intended to be distinct from "terminally ill." In fact, the *Hemlock Quarterly* has many articles and letters approving suicide and euthanasia for a wide variety of nonterminal conditions. In a poll of its members, 61 percent disagreed with the statement, "life is worth living in extreme loneliness or in the absence of loved ones and close friends."[9] Hemlock officials explain that such things are printed in a spirit of open communication and do not necessarily reflect Hemlock's formal stance. Even so, they are usually not accompanied by editorial commentary in keeping with Hemlock's stated principles.

The more recent writings of Hemlock's founder, Derek Humphry, reveal that the concept of terminal illness has now expanded to embrace such conditions as Alzheimer's disease and even osteoporosis.[10] In an article by Humphry entitled "Mrs. Bouvia's Sad Mistakes are Lessons," the author states that Bouvia's sad mistakes were that she undermined her plan by admitting herself to a hospital and attracting publicity.[11] Elsewhere, Humphry also advocates a "right" of quadriplegics to receive euthanasia.[12]

Concerning double suicide pacts, Humphry maintains that "[t]here can be no firm rules on this subject. No two sets of circumstances are alike. When all is said and done, it is an extremely personal decision. There must, we think, be a tolerance for those people who have been partners for many years and now cannot bear the thought of life without their spouse."[13] Along similar lines, Ann Wickett (Humphry's present wife and editor of the *Hemlock Quarterly*) wrote concerning Cynthia Koestler, fifty-five, who was in perfect health at the time she killed herself following her husband's suicide: "For a man in grave and failing health, self-deliverance was the final right. For Cynthia, it was the final act of devotion. That too was her right. One regrets, however, less the nature of her death, than the nature of her life."[14]

The above clearly illustrate a gravitation within Hemlock toward "euthanasia on demand." As Humphry succinctly wrote: "When should it be done? We are only here once (or so I believe) and it is folly to leave too soon. Decide what is [sic] the criteria for an acceptable quality of life for *you.*"[15]

Although Concern for Dying cultivates a considerably more moderate public image than Hemlock, the difference seems to be more one of tactic than of goal. A letter, written in 1978 by Executive Director A.-J. Rock-Levinson (now A.-J. Levinson) in response to an inquiry, revealed the wedge principle in action: "You are right when you say that our people believe rational suicide to be acceptable. . . . We also know from experience that if we try to foist our ideas too strongly and too soon on a society not yet ready to consider them, we will damage if not destroy our effectiveness. By moving cautiously and without stridency . . . we gain a larger audience for our views. On the subject of crisis centers for potential suicides, or the granting of access to lethal substances, we feel that the time is not yet right to take a public position."[16]

That euthanasia on demand is the unstated goal of the euthanasia movement should not be surprising, because (1) emotional pain is as real as, and can be worse than, physical pain, and (2) self-determination and "situation ethics" are the guiding principles. Joseph

Fletcher stated "[e]very one of these pragmatic objections [to suicide] proves . . . to be false in a great many cases. . . . [I]f our ethics is humane, . . . we'll look at every case on its own merits and refuse to be bound indiscriminately by universal rules of right and wrong, whether they claim to rest on religious or pragmatic grounds."[17] This obviously includes any rule that would restrict self-determination arbitrarily to cases of terminal illness, to say nothing of restricting "terminal illness" arbitrarily to death within six months.

The Dutch understand this perfectly well. When the Rotterdam Criminal Court legalized active voluntary euthanasia in 1981, it stipulated that the recipient need not be terminally ill; in Holland, "paraplegics can request and get aid-in-dying."[18] In fact, in the very first issue of the *Hemlock Quarterly,* under the boldfaced caption "EUTHANASIA ON DEMAND," it is reported that at the World Voluntary Euthanasia Conference in 1980, "[r]epresentatives from the three Dutch voluntary euthanasia groups surprised the conference by saying that euthanasia was available virtually 'on demand' in Holland," a situation described by the *Hemlock Quarterly* as "advanced."[19]

A Historical Analogue: The Expanding Indications for Abortion

Euthanasia advocates frequently allude to a close relationship between euthanasia and abortion.[20] If the analogy is valid, then it ironically undermines their claim that the scope of indications for legalized euthanasia would not expand beyond terminal illness. Regardless of one's views on the ethics of abortion, it is an evident historical fact that the scope of indications for it has expanded tremendously since its legalization one and a half decades ago. Although the main indications stressed by legalization proponents in the early 1970s were rape, incest, or danger to the mother's health, now as many as 99 percent of the 1.5 million annual abortions in the United States are performed for reasons of economics or convenience.[21] Moreover, the upper limit of gestational age has crept well beyond "viability," and abortion on demand at any time up to term is effectively legal in many states.[22]

The tendency of indications for legalized killing to expand is nowhere better evidenced than in the disillusionment of Chief Justice Warren Burger, who had cast a favorable vote in *Roe* v. *Wade,* yet strongly dissented in [a 1986] U.S. Supreme Court abortion decision. On July 11, 1986, the Court struck down a Pennsylvania statute requiring that women seeking abortions be informed about the relative risks of the procedure and about available support agencies if they decided to give birth. The Chief Justice stated that "every member of the *Roe* Court rejected the idea of abortion on demand. The Court's opinion today, however, plainly undermines that important principle, and I regretfully conclude that some of the concerns of the dissenting justices in *Roe,* as well as the concerns I expressed in my separate concurrence, have now been realized. . . . We have apparently already passed the point at which abortion is available merely on demand. If the statute at issue here is to be invalidated, the 'demand' will not even have to be the result of an informed choice."[23] The experience with legalized abortion, therefore, indicates it is naive to suggest that the indications for legalized euthanasia would remain forever restricted to only cases of terminal illness with great suffering.

A Further Historical Analogue: The Nazi "Euthanasia" Program

Euthanasia advocates reject the Nazi analogy on the basis that the Nazi "euthanasia" program was neither benevolent nor voluntary on the part of the recipient, and thus it was anything but euthanasia in the true sense.[24] Moreover, they contend that the excesses of a genocide program could not possibly occur in a democracy. But the meaningful analogy lies rather with the approach to medical care for Germany's own Aryan patients. Many do not realize that the first gas chambers were set up, not in concentration camps, but in hospitals, and were first used, not on Jews, but on sick Aryans. In fact, in the beginning, sick Jews were considered unworthy to receive the "benefit" of "euthanasia."[25] Of course, this "euthanasia" was entirely involuntary, but, for the moment, the focus is on the dimension of "indications for candidacy."

It is important to realize that euthanasia (in what the right-to-die organizations would consider the true, benevolent sense) had gained acceptance in substantial sectors of the German society and medical profession long before Hitler's assumption of power in 1933. As early as 1920, jurist Karl Binding and psychiatrist Alfred Hoche had published a highly influential book entitled *The Permission to Destroy Life Not Worth Living,* in which euthanasia was advocated for those suffering from incurable physical and mental illnesses, and severely retarded and defective children.[26] Emphasis was placed on "death assistance," patient consent (either explicit or by proxy), compassion, quality of life, and cost containment, concepts not unfamiliar in modern health care.[27] The book was so popular that a second printing was required only two years later,[28] and its concept of "life not worth living" became the philosophical basis for future developments in German medical/ethical thinking.

Euthanasia was increasingly discussed in academic circles during the 1920s, particularly in medical and law schools, and considerable public sympathy for it developed. Even prior to Hitler's authorization of euthanasia in 1939, some parents of infants with severe disabilities had already been seeking "mercy deaths" for their children and were pleased by the Führer's personal interest in their cases.[29] Significantly, Hitler's authorization was not so much a command but an extension of "the authority of physicians . . . so that a mercy death may be granted to patients who according to human judgment are incurably ill according to the most critical evaluation of the state of their disease."[30] Even as late as 1944, severely malformed adults were being brought in for "euthanasia" at the request of their families.[31]

The euthanasia propaganda then was essentially no different from what it is now. One of the movies popular then featured a woman with multiple sclerosis whose physician husband "finally kills her to the accompaniment of soft piano music rendered by a sympathetic colleague in an adjoining room."[32] There was a continuing reference to the costs of caring for the handicapped, retarded, and insane. The purpose behind such propaganda was to facilitate the ongoing program of involuntary "euthanasia." But the point here is that—whether voluntary or involuntary—the indications for legalized killing naturally expand. Eventually patients with minor deformities, the mildly senile, amputee war veterans, "problem children," bed-wetters, and the like were being selected by physicians on their own initiative for "mercy deaths."[33]

This expansion of criteria was not forced upon the doctors by the Nazi regime, but evolved according to its own dynamic within the medical profession, as evidenced by several facts. First, doctors who did not want to participate in the "euthanasia" program were able to continue their practice of medicine undisturbed.[34] Second, although the regime had a perverse interest in ridding German society of "useless eaters," it would hardly have perceived the lives of such basically healthy patients as detrimental either to the war effort or to its mystical quest for genetic purification. Third, the liberalization of indications actually became most wanton after Hitler had officially ended the "euthanasia" project in 1941 (in fact, the selection and killing by doctors of such minimally sick patients, for neither racial nor ideological reasons, continued in full swing right up to the end of the war, and in some places even a few days thereafter).[35]

A Contemporary Case in Point:
Legalized Euthanasia in the Netherlands

The claim that legalized euthanasia in this country will go no further than voluntary euthanasia for competent adults destined to die within six months ignores not only the lessons of history but also what is currently taking place in Holland. Since its inception there at the beginning of this decade, legalized euthanasia has evolved with surprising rapidity. "Dutch courts have steadily expanded the circumstances in which a doctor may avoid prosecution if he kills—with case law now permitting euthanasia for patients with such nonterminal afflictions as multiple sclerosis or simply the physical ravages of old age." There has been infighting between radical and moderate factions within the euthanasia movement itself, with the radicals recently prevailing. The Royal Dutch Medical Association has endorsed euthanasia on demand not only for competent adults, but also even for minors without parental consent. Advocates are now reasoning that patients with incurable psychiatric illnesses ought to be able to receive euthanasia upon request, in spite of their lack of mental competence.[36]

The situation has evolved so far in such a short period of time that even some of Holland's most prominent euthanasists are beginning to express fears for the future, given the obvious impotence of the legal system to deal with the already existing abuses. After performing a euthanasia, most Dutch physicians falsify the death certificate to reflect a "natural death," so as to minimize the likelihood of an investigation of the case. The number of complaints of suggested abuse reported to authorities rose from twelve in 1986 to twenty-four during the first half of 1987, and this is undoubtedly only the tip of an iceberg. One Dutch physician has reported that involuntary euthanasia has become so rampant and is so overlooked by the courts that elderly patients are afraid to be hospitalized or even to consult doctors.[37] The Netherlands is, therefore, demonstrating the reality, the steepness, and the slipperiness of the "slippery slope" of legalized euthanasia. It would be advisable to await the final outcome of their drastic social experiment before embarking along the same irreversible path. . . .

WHY INVOLVE PHYSICIANS?

Even if the acceptance of euthanasia did not entail all the above problems and were desirable for society, there would still be no reason to involve physicians in it, and many reasons not to. To kill someone (even gently) does not require any medical knowledge. The main reason that physicians are supposedly needed is that the "best" drugs are all prescription drugs. But what about the case of Dr. Julius Hackethal, a Gernam oncologist and contemporary hero of the euthanasia movement, who provided one of his terminal patients with an appropriately lethal amount of potassium cyanide?[38] Cyanide is hardly a prescription drug, even in Germany, and anyone can look up its lethal dose in a toxicology book. The Hemlock Society discourages this method, however, because a cyanide death, though quick, is somewhat unpleasant. It therefore recommends sedative drugs as first choice. Still, it could just as well argue that these drugs be made nonprescription, or that specially certified euthanasists be allowed to establish their own clinics, without having to involve the medical profession at all. Any patient would then have the right to transfer himself from a hospital to the nearest euthanasia center.

It would seem, therefore, that the real reason for Hemlock's insistence on *physician*-assisted suicide is to lend an air of respectability and credibility to its cause. Lifton, in his recent book on the Nazi doctors,[39] emphasized that the maintenance of a facade of respectability was precisely the reason that the Nazi regime insisted so much on having *doctors* "select" the recipients for "special treatment," operate the gas chambers, falsify death certificates to resemble natural causes, and in general maintain an aura of medicalization in every aspect of the genocide program.

The advocates of euthanasia attempt to use the medical profession for their own purposes, without regard to the irreparable harm that would be done to society by transforming the public image of physician from healer to killer, which could only undermine the covenant of trust at the very heart of the doctor-patient relationship. If this were not the case, there would be no need for the existing strong policies against physician participation in other legal forms of killing, such as capital punishment.[40] As one article stated "this new method of capital punishment [le:hal drug injected by physicians] . . . presents the most serious and intimate challenge in modern American history to active medical participation in state-ordered killings of human beings. . . . [T]his procedure requires the direct application of biomedical knowledge and skills in a corruption and exploitation of the healing profession's role in society."[41]

CONCLUSION

For all these reasons, efforts to promote death with dignity would be more appropriately channeled in the direction of physician education with regard to care of the dying, research to improve methods of symptomatic relief, and provision by society of improved resources for the persons who are disabled, chronically ill, or dying—particularly the establishment of hospices. It is unnecessary to kill these people in order to provide them with comfort and compassion; much less should physicians be the ones to kill them.

NOTES

1. Gerald Larue, "Some Social Aspects of Terminal Illness," in *Let Me Die Before I Wake,* edited by Derek Humphry (Los Angeles: Hemlock Society, 1984).

2. President's Commission for the Study of Ethical Problems in Medicine and Biomedical and Behavioral Research, *Deciding to Forego Life-Sustaining Treatment* (1983), pp. 29-30 [hereinafter President's Commission].

3. Only the first of these dimensions is included in this edited version—Eds.

4. "The Hemlock Manifesto. Towards Accepting Voluntary Euthanasia," *Hemlock Quarterly* I.C.A. (1982). Reprinted in *Let Me Die Before I Wake,* edited by Derek Humphry [hereinafter "Hemlock Manifesto"].

5. Personal communication with Dr. Ira J. Bates, Director of Education Services, National Hospice Organization.

6. *Assisted Suicide, The Compassionate Crime,* edited by Derek Humphry (Los Angeles: Hemlock Society, 1982).

7. "Hemlock Manifesto," *supra* note 4, at sec. 1.c.B.

8. See e.g., sidebar for book advertisements, *Hemlock Quarterly* 10 (1983): 6.

9. *Who Believes in Voluntary Euthanasia? A Survey of Hemlock Society Members,* Edited by M. Surber, V. Quinn, and D. Wilner (Los Angeles, The Hemlock Society, 1983), p. 22.

10. Derek Humphry and Ann Wickett, *The Right to Die: Understanding Euthanasia* (New York: Harper and Row, 1986), p. 313; Humphry, "Mercy Denied to Roswell Gilbert," *Euthanasia Review* 1 (1986): 16, 17.

11. Derek Humphry, "Mrs. Bouvia's Sad Mistakes Are Lessons," *Hemlock Quarterly* 14 (1984): 1.

12. Derek Humphry, "The Suicide Shambles" (book review), *Hemlock Quarterly* 7 (1982): 3; Humphry and Wickett, *supra* note 10, pp. 145-161.

13. Derek Humphry, "Enigma of Double Suicide," *Hemlock Quarterly* 13 (1983): 1.

14. Ann Wickett, "Why Cynthia Koestler Joined Arthur," *Hemlock Quarterly* 18 (January 1985): 4-5.

15. Derek Humphry, *Let Me Die Before I Wake* (3rd ed., 1984) (emphasis in the original).

16. P. Marx, *And Now . . . Euthanasia* (2nd ed. 1985), p. 23.

17. Joseph Fletcher, "Judge Every Case on Its Merits," *Hemlock Quarterly* 13 (1983): 4.

18. Van Till, "Dutch Doctors Get Guidelines," *Hemlock Quarterly* 17 (1984): 1, 12.

19. Note, "World Conference," *Hemlock Quarterly* 1 (1980): 1-2.

20. Note, "Abortion Scrap Over: Now It's Euthanasia," *Hemlock Quarterly* 14 (1984): 1; Joseph Fletcher, "The 'Right' to Live and the 'Right' to Die: A Protestant View of Euthanasia," *The Humanist* 34 (1974): 12-15.

21. The U.S. Senate Committee on the Judiciary, Human Life Federalism Amendment, S. Rep. No 465, 97th Cong., 2d Sess., 50 n. 256 (1982).

22. Ibid., p. 3. In a highly publicized California incident, for example, many viable fetuses were among the nearly 17,000 found in a trash container. See Jones, "Stored Fetuses to be Studied Individually," *Los Angeles Times* (May 27, 1982): Part II.

23. *Thornburgh* v. *American College of Obstetricians and Gynecologists,* 47 U.S.____, 106 S. Ct. 2169, 2190-91 (1986) (Burger, C.J., dissenting).

24. Derek Humphry and Ann Wickett, *supra* note 10, at pp. 20-32.

25. F. Wertham, *A Sign for Cain: An Exploration of Human Violence* (1973):156.

26. Karl Binding and Alfred Hoche, *Die Freigabe der Vernichtung Lebensunwerten Leben: Ihr Mass und Ihre Form (The Permission to Destroy*

Life Not Worth Living: Its Extent and Its Form) (1920), reviewed in "The Right of Putting Incurable Patients Out of the Way," *Journal of the American Medical Association* 75 (1920): 1283.

27. F. Wertham, *supra* note 25, pp. 157-159; R. Lifton, *The Nazi Doctors: Medical Killing and the Psychology of Genocide* (New York: Basic Books, 1986), pp. 46, 47.

28. F. Wertham, *supra* note 25, at p. 157.

29. R. Lifton, *supra* note 27, at pp. 50, 51.

30. F. Wertham, *supra* note 25, at p. at 162.

31. R. Lifton, *supra* note 27, at p. 97, note.

32. Alexander, "Medical Science Under Dictatorship," *The New England Journal of Medicine* 241 (1949):39. R. Lifton, *supra* note 27, at p. 49.

33. F. Wertham, *supra* note 25, at pp. 155, 156, 175.

34. Ibid., p. 161; R. Lifton, *supra* note 27, at pp. 108, 109.

35. F. Wertham, *supra* note 25, pp. 177-180; R. Lifton, supra note 27, pp. 56, 102.

36. Parchini, "The Netherlands Debates the Legal Limits of Euthanasia." *Los Angeles Times* (July 5, 1987): Part VI, at pp. 1, 8, 9.

37. Ibid.; Fenigsen, "Involuntary Euthanasia in Holland," *Wall Street Journal* (September 29, 1987): 29.

38. "German Euthanasia Case," *Hemlock Quarterly* 17 (1984): 2.

39. R. Lifton, *supra* note 26.

40. Council on Ethical and Judicial Affairs, "Current Opinions of the Council on Ethical and Judicial Affairs of the American Medical Association—1986 Sec. 2.06 (1986).

41. Curran and Casscells, "The Ethics of Medical Participation in Capital Punishment by Intravenous Drug Injection," *The New England Journal of Medicine* 302 (1980): 226-230.

16

Ethical Issues in Aiding the Death of Young Children

H. Tristram Engelhardt, Jr.

Euthanasia in the pediatric age group involves a constellation of issues that are materially different from those of adult euthanasia.[1] The difference lies in the somewhat obvious fact that infants and young children are not able to decide about their own futures and thus are not persons in the same sense that normal adults are. While adults usually decide their own fate, others decide on behalf of young children. Although one can argue that euthanasia is or should be a personal right, the sense of such an argument is obscure with respect to children. Young children do not have any personal rights, at least none that they can exercise on their own behalf with regard to the manner of their life and death. As a result, euthanasia of young children raises special questions concerning the standing of the rights of children, the status of parental rights, the obligations of adults to prevent the suffering of children, and the possible effects on society of allowing or expediting the death of seriously defective infants.

What I will refer to as the euthanasia of infants and young children might be termed by others infanticide, while some cases might be termed the withholding of extraordinary life-prolonging treatment.[2]

From *Beneficient Euthanasia,* edited by Marvin Kohl (Buffalo, N.Y.: Prometheus Books, 1975).

One needs a term that will encompass both death that results from active intervention and death that ensues when one simply ceases further therapy.[3] In using such a term, one must recognize that death is often not directly but only obliquely intended. That is, one often intends only to treat no further, not actually to have death follow, even though one knows death will follow.[4]

Finally, one must realize that deaths as the result of withholding treatment constitute a significant proportion of neonatal deaths. For example, as high as 14 percent of children in one hospital have been identified as dying after a decision was made not to treat further, the presumption being that the children would have lived longer had treatment been offered.[5]

Even popular magazines have presented accounts of parental decisions not to pursue treatment.[6] These decisions often involve a choice between expensive treatment with little chance of achieving a full, normal life for the child and "letting nature take its course," with the child dying as a result of its defects. As this suggests, many of these problems are products of medical progess. Such children in the past would have died. The quandries are in a sense an embarrassment of riches; now that one *can* treat such defective children, *must* one treat them? And, if one need not treat such defective children, may one expedite their death?

I will here briefly examine some of these issues. First, I will review differences that contrast the euthanasia of adults to the euthanasia of children. Second, I will review the issue of the rights of parents and the status of children. Third, I will suggest a new notion, the concept of the "injury of continued existence," and draw out some of its implications with respect to a duty to prevent suffering. Finally, I will outline some important questions that remain unanswered even if the foregoing issues can be settled. In all, I hope more to display the issues involved in a difficult question than to advance a particular set of answers to particular dilemmas.

For the purpose of this [chapter], I will presume that adult euthanasia can be justified by an appeal to freedom. In the face of imminent death, one is usually choosing between a more painful and more protracted dying and a less painful or less protracted dying, in circumstances where either choice makes little difference with regard to the discharge of social duties and responsibilities. In the case of suicide, we might argue that, in general, social duties (for example, the duty to support one's family) restrain one from taking one's own life. But in the face of imminent death and in the presence of the pain and deterioration of a fatal disease, such duties are usually impossible to discharge and are thus rendered moot. One can, for example, picture an extreme case of an adult with a widely disseminated carcinoma, including metastases to the brain, who because of severe pain and debilitation is no longer capable of discharging any social duties. In these and similar circumstances, euthanasia becomes the issue of the right to control one's own body, even to the point of seeking assistance in suicide. Euthanasia is, as such, the issue of assisted suicide, the universalization of a maxim that all persons should be free, *in extremis,* to decide with regard to the circumstances of their death.

Further, the choice of positive euthanasia could be defended as the more rational choice: the choice of a less painful death and the affirmation of the value of a rational life. In so choosing, one would be acting to set limits to one's life in order not to live when pain and physical and mental deterioration make further rational life impossible. The choice to end one's life can be understood as a non-contradictory willing of a smaller set of states of existence for oneself, a set that would not include a painful death. As such, it would not involve a desire to destroy oneself. That is, adult euthanasia can be construed as an affirmation of the rationality and autonomy of the self.[7]

The remarks above focus on the active or positive euthanasia of adults. But they hold as well concerning what is often called passive or negative euthanasia, the refusal of life-prolonging therapy. In such cases, the patient's refusal of life-prolonging therapy is seen to be a right that derives from personal freedom, or at least from a zone of privacy into which there are no good grounds for social intervention.[8]

Again, none of these considerations apply directly to the euthanasia of young children, because they cannot participate in such decisions. Whatever else pediatric, in particular neonatal, euthanasia involves, it surely involves issues different from those of adult euthanasia. Since infants and small children cannot commit suicide, their right to assisted suicide is difficult to pose. The difference between the euthanasia of young children and that of adults resides in the difference between children and adults. The difference, in fact, raises the troublesome question of whether young children are persons, or at least whether they are persons in the sense in which adults are. Answering that question will resolve in part at least the right of others to decide whether a young child should live or die and whether he should receive life-prolonging treatment.

THE STATUS OF CHILDREN

Adults belong to themselves in the sense that they are rational and free and therefore responsible for their actions. Adults are *sui juris*. Young children, though, are neither self-possessed nor responsible. While adults exist in and for themselves, as self-directive and self-conscious beings, young children, especially newborn infants, exist for their families and those who love them. They are not, nor can they in any sense be, responsible for themselves. If being a person is to be a responsible agent, a bearer of rights and duties, children are not persons in a strict sense. They are, rather, persons in a social sense: others must act on their behalf and bear responsibility for them. They are, as it were, entities defined by their place in social roles (for example, mother-child, family-child) rather than beings that define themselves as persons, that is, in and through themselves. Young children live as persons in and through the care of those who are responsible for them, and those responsible for them exercise the children's rights on their behalf. In this sense children belong to families in ways that most adults do not. They exist in and through their family and society.

Treating young children with respect has, then, a sense different from treating adults with respect. One can respect neither a newborn infant's or a very young child's wishes nor its freedom. In fact, a newborn infant or young child is more an entity that is valued highly because it will grow to be a person and because it plays a social role as if it were a person.[9] That is, a small child is treated as if it were a person in social roles such as mother-child and family-child relationships, though strictly speaking the child is in no way capable of claiming or being responsible for the rights imputed to it. All the rights and duties of the child are exercised and "held in trust" by others for a future time and for a person yet to develop.

Medical decisions to treat or not to treat a neonate or small child often turn on the probability and cost of achieving that future status—a developed personal life. The usual practice of letting anencephalic children (who congenitally lack all or most of the brain) die can be understood as a decision based on the absence of the possibility of achieving a personal life. The practice of refusing treatment to at least some children born with meningomyelocele can be justified through a similar, but more utilitarian, calculus. In the case of anencephalic children one might argue that care for them as persons is futile since they will never be persons. In the case of a child with meningomyelocele, one might argue that when the cost of cure would likely be very high and the probable lifestyle open to attainment very truncated, there is not a positive duty to make a large investment of money and suffering. One should note that the cost here must include not only financial costs but also the anxiety and suffering that prolonged and uncertain treatment of the child would cause the parents.

This further raises the issue of the scope of positive duties not only when there is no person present in a strict sense, but when the likelihood of a full human life is also very uncertain. Clinical and parental judgment may and should be guided by the expected lifestyle and the cost (in parental and societal pain and money) of its attainment. The decision about treatment, however, belongs properly to the parents because the child belongs to them in a sense that it does not belong to anyone else, even to itself. The care and raising of the child falls to the parents, and when considerable cost and little prospect of reasonable success are present, the parents may properly decide against life-prolonging treatment.

The physician's role is to present sufficient information in a usable form to the parents to aid them in making a decision. The accent is on the absence of a positive duty to treat in the presence of severe inconvenience (costs) to the parents; treatment that is very costly is not obligatory. What is suggested here is a general notion that there is never a duty to engage in extraordinary treatment and that "extraordinary" can be defined in terms of costs. This argument concerns children (1) whose future quality of life is likely to be seriously compromised and (2) whose present treatment would be very costly. The issue is that of the circumstances under which parents would not be obliged to take on severe burdens on behalf of their children or those circumstances under which society would not be so obliged. The argument would hold as well for those cases where the expected future life would surely be of normal quality, though its attainment would be extremely costly. The fact of little likelihood of success in attaining a normal life for the child makes decisions to do without treatment more plausible because the hope of success is even more remote and therefore the burden borne by parents or society becomes in that sense more extraordinary. But very high costs themselves could be a sufficient criterion, though in actual cases judgments in that regard would be very difficult when a normal life could be expected.[10]

The decisions in these matters correctly lie in the hands of the parents, because it is primarily in terms of the family that children exist and develop—until children become persons strictly, they are persons in virtue of their social roles. As long as parents do not unjustifiably neglect the humans in those roles so that the value and purpose of that role (that is, child) stands to be eroded (thus endangering other children), society need not intervene. In short, parents may decide for or against the treatment of their severely deformed children.

However, society has a right to intervene and protect children for whom parents refuse care (including treatment) when such care does not constitute a severe burden and when it is likely that the child could be brought to a good quality of life. Obviously, "severe burden" and "good quality of life" will be difficult to define and their meanings will vary, just as it is always difficult to say when grains of sand dropped on a table constitute a heap. At most, though, society need only intervene when the grains clearly do not constitute a heap, that is, when it is clear that the burden is light and the chance of a good quality of life for the child is high. A small child's dependence on his parents is so essential that society need intervene only when the absence of intervention would lead to the role "child" being undermined. Society must value mother-child and family-child relationships and should intervene only in cases where (1) neglect is unreasonable and therefore would undermine respect and care for children, or (2) where societal intervention would prevent children from suffering unnecessary pain.[11]

THE INJURY OF CONTINUED EXISTENCE

But there is another viewpoint that must be considered: that of the child or even the person the child might become. It might be argued that the child has a right not to have its life prolonged. The idea that forcing existence on a child could be wrong is a difficult notion, which, if true, would serve to amplify the foregoing argument. Such an argument would allow the construal of the issue in terms of the perspective of the child, that is, in terms of a duty not to treat in the circumstances where treatment would only prolong suffering. In particular, it would at least give a framework for a decision to stop treatment in cases where, though the costs of treatment are not high, the child's existence would be characterized by severe pain and deprivation.

A basis for speaking of continuing existence as an injury to the child is suggested by the proposed legal concept of "wrongful life." A number of suits have been initiated in the United States and in other countries on the grounds that life or existence itself is, under certain circumstances, a tort or injury to the living person.[12] Although thus far all such suits have ultimately failed, some have succeeded in their initial stages. Two examples may be instructive. In each case the ability to receive recompense for the injury (the tort) presupposed the existence of the individual, whose existence was itself the injury. In one case a suit was initiated on behalf of a child against his father alleging that his father's siring of him out of wedlock was an injury to the child.[13] In another case a suit on behalf of a child born of an inmate of a state mental hospital impregnated by rape in that institution was brought against the state of New York.[14] The suit was brought on the grounds that being born with such historical antecedents was itself an injury for which recovery was due. Both cases presupposed that nonexistence would have been preferable to the conditions under which the person born was forced to live.

The suits for tort for wrongful life raise the issue not only of when it would be preferable not to have been born but also of when it would be *wrong* to cause a person to be born. This implies that someone should have judged that it would have been preferable for the child never to have had existence, never to have been in the position to judge that the particular circumstances of life were intolerable.[15] Further, it implies that the person's existence under those circumstances should have been prevented and that, not having been prevented, life was not a gift but an injury. The concept of tort for wrongful life raises an issue concerning the responsibility for giving another person existence, namely, the notion that giving life is not always necessarily a good and justifiable action. Instead, in certain circumstances, so it has been argued, one may have a duty *not* to give existence to another person. This concept involves the claim that certain qualities of life have a negative value, making life an injury, not a gift; it involves, in short, a concept of human accountability and responsibility for human life. It contrasts with the notion that life is a gift of God and thus similar to other "acts of God," (that is, events for which no man is accountable). The concept thus signals the fact that humans can now control reproduction and that where rational control is possible humans are accountable. That is, the expansion of human capabilities has resulted in an expansion of human responsibilities such that one must now decide when and under what circumstances persons will come into existence.

The concept of tort for wrongful life is transferable in part to the painfully compromised existence of children who can only have their life prolonged for a short, painful, and marginal existence. The concept suggests that allowing life to be prolonged under such circumstances would itself be an injury of the person whose painful and severely compromised existence would be made to continue. In fact, it suggests that there is a duty not to prolong life if it can be determined to have a substantial negative value for the person involved.[16] Such issues are moot in the case of adults, who can and should decide for themselves. But small children cannot make such a choice. For them it is an issue of justifying prolonging life under circumstances of painful and compromised existence. Or, put differently, such cases indicate the need to develop social canons to allow a decent death for children for whom the only possibility is protracted, painful suffering.

I do not mean to imply that one should develop a new basis for civil damages. In the field of medicine, the need is to recognize an ethical category, a concept of wrongful continuance of existence, not a new legal right. The concept of injury for continuance of existence, the proposed analogue of the concept of the tort for wrongful life, presupposes that life can be of a negative value such that the medical maxim *primum non nocere* ("first do no harm") would require not sustaining life.[17]

The idea of responsibility for acts that sustain or prolong life is cardinal to the notion that one should not under certain circumstances further prolong the life of a child. Unlike adults, children cannot decide with regard to euthanasia (positive or negative), and if more than a utilitarian justification is sought, it must be sought in a duty not to inflict life on another person in circumstances where that life would be painful and futile. This position must rest on the facts that (1) medicine now can cause the prolongation of the life of seriously deformed children who in the past would have died young and that (2) it is not clear that life so prolonged is a good for the child. Further, the choice is made not on the basis of costs to the parents or to society but on the basis of the child's suffering and compromised existence.

The difficulty lies in determining what makes life not worth living for a child. Answers could never be clear. It seems reasonable, however, that the life of children with diseases that involve pain and no hope of survival should not be prolonged. In the case of Tay-Sachs disease (a disease marked by a progressive increase in spasticity and dementia usually leading to death at age three or four), one can hardly imagine that the terminal stages of spastic reaction to stimuli and great difficulty in swallowing are at all pleasant to the child (even insofar as it can only minimally perceive its circumstances). If such a child develops aspiration pneumonia and is treated, it can reasonably be said that to prolong its life is to inflict suffering. Other diseases give fairly clear portraits of lives not worth living: for example, Lesch-Nyhan disease, which is marked by mental retardation and compulsive self-mutilation.

The issue is more difficult in the case of children with diseases for whom the prospects for normal intelligence and a fair lifestyle do exist, but where these chances are remote and their realization expensive. Children born with meningomyelocele present this dilemma. Imagine, for example, a child that falls within Lorber's fifth category (an IQ of sixty or less, sometimes blind, subject to [seizures], and always incontinent). Such a child has little prospect of anything approaching a normal life, and there is a good chance of its dying even with treatment.[18] But such judgments are statistical. And if one does not treat such children, some will still survive and, as John Freeman indicates, be worse off if not treated.[19] In such cases one is in a dilemma. If one always treats, one must justify extending the life of those who will ultimately die anyway and in the process subjecting them to the morbidity of multiple surgical procedures. How remote does the prospect of a good life have to be in order not to be worth great pain and expense?[20] It is probably best to decide, in the absence of a positive duty to treat, on the basis of the cost and suffering to parents and society. But, as Freeman argues, the prospect of prolonged or even increased suffering raises the issue of active euthanasia.[21]

If the child is not a person strictly, and if death is inevitable and expediting it would diminish the child's pain prior to death, then it would seem to follow that, all else being equal, a decision for active euthanasia would be permissible, even obligatory.[22] The difficulty lies with "all else being equal," for it is doubtful that active euthanasia could be established as a practice without eroding and endangering children generally, since, as John Lorber has pointed out, children cannot speak in their own behalf.[23] Thus, although there is no argument in principle against the active euthanasia of small children, there could be an argument against such practices based on questions of prudence. To put it another way, even though one might have a duty to hasten the death of a particular child, one's duty to protect children in general could override that first duty. The issue of active euthanasia turns in the end on whether it would have social consequences that refraining would not, on whether (1) it is possible to establish procedural safeguards for limited active euthanasia and (2) whether such practices would have a significant adverse effect on the treatment of small children in general. But since these are procedural issues dependent on sociological facts, they are not open to an answer within the confines of this [chapter]. In any event, the concept of the injury of continued existence provides a basis for the justification of the passive euthanasia of small children—a practice already widespread and somewhat established in our society—beyond the mere absence of a positive duty to treat.[24]

CONCLUSION

Though the lack of certainty concerning questions such as the prognosis of particular patients and the social consequence of active euthanasia of children prevents a clear answer to all the issues raised by the euthanasia of infants, it would seem that this much can be maintained: (1) Since children are not persons strictly but exist in and through their families, parents are the appropriate ones to decide whether or not to treat a deformed child when (a) there is not only little likelihood of full human life but also great likelihood of suffering if life is prolonged, or (b) when the cost of prolonging life is very great. Such decisions must be made in consort with a physician who will be able to help the parents with the consequences of their decision. (2) It is reasonable to speak of a duty not to treat a small child when such treatment will only prolong a painful life or would in any event lead to a painful death. Though this does not by any means answer all the questions, it does point out an important fact—that medicine's duty is not always to prolong life doggedly but sometimes is quite the contrary.

NOTES

1. I am grateful to Laurence B. McCullough and James P. Morris for their critical discussion of this paper. They may be responsible for its virtues, but not for its shortcomings.

2. The concept of extraordinary treatment as it has been developed in Catholic moral theology is useful: treatment is extraordinary and therefore not obligatory if it involves great costs, pain, or inconvenience, and is a grave burden to oneself or others without a reasonable expectation that such treatment would be successful. See Gerald Kelly, S.J., *Medico-Moral Problems* (St. Louis: The Catholic Hospital Association Press, 1958), pp. 128-141. Difficulties are hidden in such terms as "great costs" and "reasonable expectation," as well as in terms such as "successful." Such ambiguity reflects the fact that precise operational definitions are not available. That is, the precise meaning of "great," "reasonable," and "successful" are inextricably bound to particular circumstances, especially particular societies.

3. I will use the term euthanasia in a broad sense to indicate a deliberately chosen course of action or inaction that is known at the time of the decision to be such as will expedite death. This use of euthanasia will encompass not only positive or active euthanasia (acting in order to expedite death) and negative or passive euthanasia (refraining from action in order to expedite death), but acting and refraining in the absence of a direct intention that death occur more quickly (that is, those cases that fall under the concept of double effect). See note 4.

4. But, both active and passive euthanasia can be appreciated in terms of the Catholic moral notion of double effect. When the doctrine of double effect is invoked, one is strictly not intending euthanasia, but rather one intends something else. That concept allows actions or omissions that lead

to death (1) because it is licit not to prolong life *in extremis* (allowing death is not an intrinsic evil), (2) if death is not actually willed or actively sought (that is, the evil is not directly willed), (3) if that which is willed is a major good (for example, avoiding useless major expediture of resources or serious pain), and (4) if the good is not achieved by means of the evil (for example, one does not will to save resources or diminish pain *by* the death). With regard to euthanasia the doctrine of double effect means that one need not expend major resources in an endeavor that will not bring health but only prolong dying and that one may use drugs that decrease pain but hasten death. See Richard McCormick, *Ambiguity in Moral Choice* (Milwaukee: Marquette University Press, 1973). I exclude the issue of double effect from my discussion because I am interested in those cases in which the good may follow directly from the evil—the death of a child. In part, though, the second section of this paper is concerned with the concept of proportionate good.

    5. Raymond S. Duff and A. G. M. Campbell, "Moral and Ethical Dilemmas in the Special-Care Nursery," *The New England Journal of Medicine* 289 (October 25, 1973): 890-894.

    6. Roger Pell, "The Agonizing Decision of Joanne and Roger Pell," *Good Housekeeping* (January 1972): 76-77, 131-135.

    7. This somewhat Kantian argument is obviously made in opposition to Kant's position that suicide involves a default of one's duty to oneself ". . . to preserve his life simply because he is a person and must therefore recognize a duty to himself (and a strict one at that)," as well as a contradictory volition: "that man ought to have the authorization to withdraw himself from all obligation, that is, to be free to act as if no authorization at all were required for this withdrawal, involves a contradiction. To destroy the subject of morality in his own person is tantamount to obliterating from the world . . ." Immanuel Kant, *The Metaphysical Principles of Virtue: Part II of the Metaphysics of Morals,* trans. James Ellington (Indianapolis: Bobbs-Merrill, 1964), p. 83; Akademie Edition, VI, 422-423.

    8. Norman L. Cantor, "A Patient's Decision to Decline Life-Saving Medical Treatment: Bodily Integrity versus the Preservation of Life," *Rutgers Law Review,* 26 (Winter 1972): 239.

    9. By "young child" I mean either an infant or a child so young as not yet to be able to participate, in any sense, in a decision. A precise operational definition of "young child" would clearly be difficult to develop. It is also not clear how one would bring older children into such decisions. See, for example, Milton Viederman, "Saying 'No' to Hemodialysis: Exploring Adaptation," and Daniel Burke, "Saying 'No' to Hemodialysis: An Acceptable Decision," both in *The Hastings Center Report,* 4 (September 1974): 8-10, and John E. Schowalter, Julian B. Ferholt, and Nancy M. Mann, "The Adolescent Patient's Decision to Die," *Pediatrics,* 51 (January 1973): 97-103.

10. An appeal to high costs alone is probably hidden in judgments based on statistics: even though there is a chance for a normal life for certain children with apparently severe cases of meningomyelocele, one is not obliged to treat since that chance is small, and the pursuit of that chance is very expensive. Cases of the costs being low but the expected suffering of the child being high will be discussed under the concept of the injury of continued existence. It should be noted that none of the arguments in this paper bear on cases where neither the cost nor the suffering of the child is considerable. Cases in this last category probably include, for example, children born with mongolism complicated only by duodenal atresia.

11. I have in mind here the issue of physicians, hospital administrators, or others being morally compelled to seek an injunction to force treatment of the child in the absence of parental consent. In these circumstances, the physician, who is usually best acquainted with the facts of the case, is the natural advocate of the child.

12. G. Tedeschi, "On Tort Liability for 'Wrongful Life,'" *Israel Law Review* 1 (1966):513.

13. *Zepeda* v. *Zepeda:* 41 Ill. App. 2d 240, 190 N.E. 2d 849 (1963).

14. *Williams* v. *State of New York:* 46 Misc. 2d 824, 260 N.Y.S. 2d 953 (Ct. Cl., 1965).

15. Torts: "Illegitimate Child Denied Recovery against Father for 'Wrongful Life,'" *Iowa Law Review* 49 (1969): 1009.

16. It is one thing to have a conceptual definition of the injury of continued existence (for example, causing a person to continue to live under circumstances of severe pain and deprivation when there are no alternatives but death) and another to have an operational definition of that concept (that is, deciding what counts as such severe pain and deprivation). This article has focused on the first, not the second, issue.

17. H. Tristram Engelhardt, Jr., "Euthanasia and Children: The Injury of Continued Existence," *The Journal of Pediatrics* 83 (July 1973): 170-171.

18. John Lorber, "Results of Treatment of Myelomeningocele," *Developmental Medicine and Child Neurology* 13 (1971): 286.

19. John M. Freeman, "The Shortsighted Treatment of Myelomeningocele: A Long-Term Case Report," *Pediatrics* 53 (March 1974): 311-313.

20. John M. Freeman, "To Treat or Not to Treat," *Practical Management of Meningomyelocele,* ed. John Freeman (Baltimore: University Park Press, 1974), p. 21.

21. John Lorber, "Selective Treatment of Myelomeningocele: To Treat or Not to Treat," *Pediatrics* 53 (March 1974): 307-308.

22. I am presupposing that no intrinsic moral distinctions exist in cases such as these, between acting and refraining, between omitting care in the hope that death will ensue (that is, rather than the child living to be even

more defective) and acting to ensure that death will ensue rather than having the child live under painful and seriously compromised circumstances. For a good discussion of the distinction between acting and refraining, see Jonathan Bennett, "Whatever the Consequences," *Analysis* 26 (January 1966): 83-102; P. J. Fitzgerald, "Acting and Refraining," *Analysis* 27 (March 1967): 133-139; Daniel Dinello, "On Killing and Letting Die," *Analysis* 31 (April 1971): 83-86.

   23. Lorber, "Selective Treatment of Myelomeningocele," p. 308.

   24. Positive duties involve a greater constraint than negative duties. Hence it is often easier to establish a duty not to do something (not to treat further) than a duty to do something (to actively hasten death). Even allowing a new practice to be permitted (for example, active euthanasia) requires a greater attention to consequences than does establishing the absence of a positive duty. For example, at common law there is no basis for action against a person who watches another drown without giving aid; this reflects the difficulty of establishing a positive duty.

17

Conclusions of a
British Medical Association Review
of Guidelines on Euthanasia

The council of the BMA has approved *The Euthanasia Report,* prepared by a working party, which was chaired by Sir Henry Yellowlees.[1] . . . The conclusions in the report are reproduced here.

Some patients see death as the fitting conclusion to the events of their life. These people may wish neither to hasten their death nor to delay it. For them, death is a mystery which they approach with tranquility. There are limits to medical science and it is inappropriate for doctors to insist on intruding in these circumstances.

There is a distinction between an active intervention by a doctor to terminate life and a decision not to prolong life (a nontreatment decision). In both of these categories there are occasions on which a patient will ask for one of these courses of action to be taken and times when the patient could say but does not. There are also occasions where the patient is incompetent to decide.

An active intervention by anybody to terminate another person's life should remain illegal. Neither doctors nor any other occupational group should be placed in a category which lessens their responsibility for their actions.

"Euthanasia: Conclusions of a BMA Working Party Set Up to Review the Association's Guidance on Euthanasia," *British Medical Journal* 296 (May 14, 1988). ISBN 0-7279-0234-2 British Medical Association.

In clinical practice there are many cases where it is right that a doctor should accede to a request not to prolong the life of the patient. Appropriate medical skills and techniques should be offered to patients when there is a good chance of providing an extension of life that will have the quality that the patient seeks.

Patient autonomy is a crucial aspect of informed patient care. This is achieved most successfully where a trusting and open relationship between the doctor and the patient allows participation in decisions about illness and its treatment. Doctors should regard patients as authorizing treatment, and should respect those authorizations and any decision to withdraw consent. But autonomy works both ways. Patients have the right to decline treatment but do not have the right to demand treatment which the doctor cannot, in conscience, provide. An active intervention by a doctor to terminate a patient's life is just such a "treatment." Patients cannot and should not be able to *require* their doctors to collaborate in their death. If a patient does make such a request there should be a presumption that the doctor will not agree.

More important than debate about the limits of autonomy is the need for doctors and everyone else who is involved in the care of the terminally ill to communicate with their dying patients. Doctors need to be able to elicit the fears of dying patients and to discuss and answer those fears. They need to be able to discuss terminal care openly so that patients can see that they will not be abandoned and left helpless in the face of a terminal disease. Only if such communication and good treatment becomes the norm can society expect to dissipate the pressure to force doctors to do things that the medical profession should not accept.

The killing of an individual who is certain to suffer severe pain and to be isolated from human warmth and compassion as they die, is held by some to be very similar to the situation of a terminally ill patient. In the hypothetical case of the person trapped in a hotel fire there may appear to be no alternative to a decision to intervene actively to end the person's life. This applies equally to the actions of army doctors in Burma in the Second World War. Today, however, terminal medical care is offered by individuals and groups dedicated to the relief of suffering and respect for the feelings and worth of the dying patient. These aims are achieved regularly and with considerable success. The two situations are not comparable.

Requests from young and severely disabled patients for a doctor's intervention to end their life present one of the hardest problems in day to day care. Counselling is essential to reaffirm the value of the person, and to counter pressure which may be created by the feeling of being unloved and an embarrassment or inconvenience to those upon whom the patient is wholly dependent. The subtle and dynamic factors surrounding disability and the wish to die make any drastic change in the law unwise for this group of patients.

Any move toward liberalizing the active termination of a severely malformed infant's life would herald a serious and incalculable change in the present ethos of medicine. Nevertheless, there are circumstances where the doctor may judge correctly that continuing to treat an infant is cruel and that the doctor should ease the baby's dying rather than prolong it by the insensitive use of medical technology.

This kind of decision requires careful communication between doctor, parents, nursing staff, and other caregivers. It is imperative that the doctor should start from a position which seeks to preserve and value life rather than, on occasion, to judge it as not worth while. It is important also to stress that withholding treatment does not preclude loving care for the dying infant. This will, of course, involve relieving the infant's distress.

An overwhelming majority of those who are rescued from serious suicide attempts do not repeat their attempts. This means that individuals who make such a choice about their own deaths do not always affirm this in the light of reflection. The techniques developed in the Netherlands mean that the opportunity for reflection is unlikely to be available to a person when a doctor acts to terminate their life.

Advance declarations of the type envisaged are not recognized as binding by English or, we believe, Scottish law. They may be a valuable guide to the wishes of a patient who can no longer participate in clinical decisions, but should not be regarded as immutable or legally binding prescriptions for medical care. They require respectful attention and sensitive interpretation.

The law's deep-seated adherence to intent rather than consequence alone is an important reference point in the moral assessment of any action. A decision to withdraw treatment which has become a burden and is no longer of continuing benefit to a patient has a different intent to one which involves ending the life of a person. We accept drug treatment which may involve a risk to the patient's life if the sole intention is to relieve illness, pain, distress, or suffering.

Any doctor, compelled by conscience to intervene to end a person's life, will do so prepared to face the closest scrutiny of this action that the law might wish to make.

The law should not be changed and the deliberate taking of a human life should remain a crime. This rejection of a change in the law to permit doctors to intervene to end a person's life is not just a subordination of individual well-being to social policy. It is, instead, an affirmation of the supreme value of the individual, no matter how worthless and hopeless that individual might feel.

NOTE

1. British Medical Association. *The Euthanasia Report*. London: BMA, 1988.

18

The Case for Active Voluntary Euthanasia

Statement Drafted by Gerald A. Larue

We, the undersigned, declare our support for the decriminalization of medically induced active euthanasia when requested by the terminally ill.

We acknowledge that techniques developed by modern medicine have been beneficial in improving the quality of life and increasing longevity, but they have sometimes been accompanied by harmful and dehumanizing effects. We are aware that many terminally ill persons have been kept alive against their will by advanced medical technologies, and that terminally ill patients have been denied assistance in dying. In attempting to terminate their suffering by ending their lives themselves or with the help of loved ones not trained in medicine, some patients have botched their suicides and brought further suffering on themselves and those around them. We believe that the time is now for society to rise above the archaic prohibitions of the past and to recognize that terminally ill individuals have the right to choose the time, place, and manner of their own death.

We respect the opinions of those who declare that only the deity should determine the moment of death, or who find some spiritual merit in suffering, but we reject their arguments. We align ourselves with those who are committed to the defense of human rights, human

From *Free Inquiry* 9, No. 1 (Winter 1988-89). Reprinted by permission of the publisher.

dignity, and human self-determination: this includes the right to die with dignity. An underlying motive is compassion for those who wish to end their suffering by hastening their moment of death.

There are those who would make a distinction between "active" and "passive" euthanasia; they would support the abandonment of "heroic" efforts to sustain life while opposing any positive act to hasten death by increasing dosage of drugs or administering a lethal injection. We point out, however, that both passive and active euthanasia involve the intention of ending a person's life.

We support only *voluntary* euthanasia. We believe that once an adult has signed a living will expressing his or her personal wishes concerning treatment during a terminal illness and/or has signed a durable power of attorney or health care statement enabling another to act on his or her behalf, the individual's wishes should be respected. Because most persons lack professional knowledge concerning methods of inducing death, we believe that only a cooperating medical doctor should be the one to administer the life-taking potion or injection to the patient who has requested it and that the doctor should be able to fulfill the patient's request without fear or threat of prosecution.

We respect the doctor's and the hospital's right to refuse to participate in administering such terminal medications. We would urge the medical profession to make clear the patient's right to change doctors and hospitals should his or her wishes for aid in dying be refused. We would urge that every effort be made to honor the terminally ill person's wishes in regard to the time and place of death, and that if the patient desires family members to be present to give comfort, these requests will be respected.

We recognize that there may be some who would exploit the right to active voluntary euthanasia and take advantage of the ill and suffering. But we believe that protective laws can, and indeed must, be enacted to discourage and punish such action.

We respect the right of terminally ill individuals who do not wish to utilize euthanasia or hasten the moment of death. But we affirm that the wishes of those who believe in the right to die with dignity should be respected and that to do so involves the highest expression of moral compassion and beneficence.

Pieter Admiraal, M.D., Anesthesiologist, Reinier de Graff Gasthuis

Bonnie Bullough, Dean of Nursing, State University of New York at Buffalo

Vern Bullough, Dean of Natural and Social Sciences, State University of New York College at Buffalo

Francis Crick, Nobel Laureate in Physiology, Salk Institute

Albert Ellis, President, Institute for Rational Emotive Therapy

Roy Fairfield, Social Scientist, Union Graduate School

Joseph Fletcher, Professor Emeritus of Medical Ethics, University of Virginia Medical School

Peter Hare, Chairman, Philosophy Department, State University of New York at Buffalo

Sidney Hook, Professor Emeritus of Philosophy, New York University

Derek Humphry, President and Chief Executive Officer, National Hemlock Society

Edna Ruth Johnson, Editor, *Churchman's Human Quest*

Marvin Kohl, Professor of Philosophy, State University of New York College at Fredonia

Helga Kuhse, Deputy Director, Monash University Centre for Human Bioethics

Paul Kurtz, Professor of Philosophy, State University of New York at Buffalo

Gerald A. Larue, Professor Emeritus of Archaeology and Biblical Studies, University of Southern California at Los Angeles

Henry Morgentaler, M.D., President, Humanist Association of Canada

Robert L. Risley, Attorney, President, Americans Against Human Suffering

B. F. Skinner, Professor of Psychology, Emeritus, Harvard University

Rob Tielman, Co-president, International Humanist and Ethical Union

Mitsuo Tomita, M.D., Assistant Clinical Professor, University of California at San Diego

19

The Physician's Responsibility toward Hopelessly Ill Patients
A Second Look

Sidney H. Wanzer, et al.

Some of the practices that were controversial five years ago[1] in the care of the dying patient have become accepted and routine. Do-not-resuscitate (DNR) orders, nonexistent only a few years ago, are now commonplace. Many physicians and ethicists now agree that there is little difference between nasogastric or intravenous hydration and other life-sustaining measures. They have concluded, therefore, that it is ethical to withdraw nutrition and hydration from certain dying, hopelessly ill, or permanently unconscious patients. The public and the courts have tended to accept this principle. Most important, there has been an increase in sensitivity to the desires of dying patients on the part of doctors, other health professionals, and the public. The entire subject is now discussed openly. Various studies and reports

From *The New England Journal of Medicine* 320, No. 13 (March 30, 1989): 844–849. Copyright 1989 Massachusetts Medical Society.

This article is jointly authored by: Sidney H. Wanzer, M.D., Daniel D. Federman, M.D., S. James Adelstein, M.D., Christine K. Cassell, M.D., Edwin H. Cassem, M.D., Ronald E. Cranford, M.D., Edward W. Hook, M.D., Bernard Lo, M.D., Charles G. Moertel, M.D., Peter Safar, M.D., Alan Stone, M.D., and Jan van Eys, Ph.D., M.D.

from governmental bodies, private foundations, the American Medical Association, and state medical societies reflect these advances in thinking.[2,9]

The increased awareness of the rights of dying patients has also been translated into new laws. Thirty-eight states now have legislation covering advance directives ("living wills"), and fifteen states specifically provide that a patient's health care spokesperson, or proxy, can authorize the withholding or withdrawal of life support.[10,11]

The courts have continued to support patients' rights and have expanded the legal concept of the right to refuse medical treatment, upholding this right in more than eighty court decisions.[12] As a general rule, the cases in the early 1980s involved terminally ill patients whose death was expected whether or not treatment was continued, and the treatment at issue—for instance, prolonged endotracheal intubation, mechanical ventilation, dialysis, or chemotherapy—was often intrusive or burdensome. The courts recognized the patient's common-law right to autonomy (to be left alone to make one's own choices) as well as the constitutional right to privacy (to be protected from unwanted invasive medical treatment).

Currently, the courts are moving closer to the view that patients are entitled to be allowed to die, whether or not they are terminally ill or suffering. Many recent cases have permitted treatment to be terminated in patients who are permanently unconscious, indicating that the right to refuse treatment can be used to put an end to unacceptable conditions even if the patients are not perceptibly suffering or close to death. In such court opinions, many of which have dealt with artificial feeding, the cause of the patient's death continues to be attributed to the underlying disease, rather than to the withholding or withdrawal of treatment.[13]

Popular attitudes about the rights of dying patients have also changed, often in advance of the attitudes of health care providers, legislators, and the courts. The results of one public-opinion poll indicated that 68 percent of the respondents believed that "people dying of an incurable painful disease should be allowed to end their lives before the disease runs its course."[14]

Health professionals have also become much more aware of patients' rights. In states with laws legitimizing living wills, hospitals have become responsive to patients' wishes as expressed in their advance directives, and hospital accreditation by the Joint Commission on Accreditation of Health Care Organizations now requires the establishment of formal DNR policies. The frequency with which DNR orders are used in nursing homes has also increased. In 1987, the California Department of Health Services became the first state agency to develop clear guidelines for the removal of life support, including tube feeding, in the state's 1,500 nursing homes and convalescent hospitals.[15]

GAPS BETWEEN ACCEPTED POLICIES AND THEIR IMPLEMENTATION

Many patients are aware of their right to make decisions about their health care, including the refusal of life-sustaining measures, yet few actually execute living wills or appoint surrogates through a health care proxy. Although such documents can be very helpful in clarifying the patient's wishes, they are all too infrequently discussed in standard medical practice. Furthermore, at present, advance directives do not exert enough influence on either the patient's ability to control medical decision making at the end of life or the physician's behavior with respect to such issues in hospitals, emergency rooms, and nursing homes. There remains a considerable gap between the acceptance of the directive and its implementation. There is also a large gap between what the courts now allow with respect to withdrawal of treatment and what physicians actually do. All too frequently, physicians are reluctant to withdraw aggressive treatment from hopelessly ill patients, despite clear legal precedent.

Physicians have a responsibility to consider timely discussions with patients about life-sustaining treatment and terminal care. Only a minority of physicians now do so consistently.[16] The best time to begin such discussions is during the course of routine, nonemergency care, remembering that not all patients are emotionally prepared, by virtue of their stage in life, their psychological makeup, or the stage of their illness. Nevertheless, as a matter of routine, physicians should become acquainted with their patients' personal values and wishes and should document them just as they document information about medical history, family history, and sociocultural background. Such discussions and the resultant documentation should be considered a part of the minimal standard of acceptable care. The physician should take the initiative in obtaining the documentation and should enter it in the medical record.

These issues are not sufficiently addressed in medical schools and residency programs. Medical educators need to recognize that practitioners may not sufficiently understand or value the patient's role in medical decision making or may be unwilling to relinquish control of the decision-making process. The interests of patients and physicians alike are best served when decisions are made jointly, and medical students and residents should learn to pursue this goal. These topics ought to be specifically included as curriculums are revised.

In general, health care institutions must recognize their obligation to inform patients of their right to participate in decisions about their medical care, including the right to refuse treatment, and should formulate institutional policies about the use of advance directives and the appointment of surrogate decision makers. Hospitals, health maintenance organizations, and nursing homes should ask patients on admission to indicate whether they have prepared a living will or designated a surrogate, It seems especially important that nursing homes require a regular review of patient preferences, with each patient's physician taking responsibility for ensuring that such information is obtained and documented. In the case of patients who lack decision-making capacity, surrogate decision makers should be identified and consulted appropriately. (We prefer the term "decision-making capacity" to "competency" because in the medical context, the patient either has or does not have the capacity to make decisions, whereas competency is a legal determination that can be made only by the courts.)

Although we advocate these approaches, we recognize that the mechanisms of appointing a surrogate and executing a living will do present certain problems. Obviously, it may happen that a surrogate appointed previously is unavailable for consultation when problems arise in the treatment of a patient who lacks decision-making capacity. In addition, there is the problem of determining what constitutes an outdated living will or surrogate appointment and how often they need to be reaffirmed. Laws in most states provide that a living will is valid until it is revoked, but patients need to be encouraged to update and reconfirm such directives from time to time.

SETTINGS FOR DYING

Home

Dying at home can provide the opportunity for quiet and privacy, dignity, and family closeness that may make death easier for the patient and provide consolation for the bereaved. Assuming that a stable and caring home environment exists, emotional and physical comfort is most often greatest at home, with family and friends nearby.

Patients and their families need reassurance that dying at home will not entail medical deprivation. They should be carefully instructed in the means of coping with possible problems, and appropriate community resources should be mobilized to assist them. The provision of care should be guided by the physician and implemented with the help of well-trained, highly motivated personnel from the hospice units that now serve many communities in this country, since home care often becomes too difficult for the family to handle alone. Hospice, a form of care in which an interdisciplinary team provides palliative and support services to both family and patient, is a concept whose time has come.

Recent cost-containment measures for expensive hospital care have given the home hospice movement considerable impetus, resulting in an emphasis on alternatives such as home care.[17] On the other hand, hospice care at home, which should be adequately financed by insurance as a cost-effective way to care for the patient, is often poorly reimbursed, and many hospice programs struggle to stay solvent. There is too much emphasis on reimbursement for high-technology care in the home, as opposed to hands-on nursing care. More adequate financing is clearly indicated for hospice and other home care providers, since it is clear that, overall, care at home usually costs much less than in other settings.

Nursing Home

When an admission to a nursing home is planned for a terminally ill patient, it is important to specify the treatment plans and goals at the outset. The nursing home should inquire about the patient's wishes with regard to life-sustaining procedures, including DNR orders and artificial nutrition and hydration. The patient should be encouraged to execute an advance directive, appoint a surrogate, or both. The possibility that it may be necessary to transfer the patient to a general hospital should be discussed in advance (transfer may become indicated, but usually it is not). All parties should anticipate that the final phases of the dying process will occur in the nursing home without a transfer to the hospital, unless the patient cannot be kept reasonably comfortable in the nursing home.

Even though care can clearly be given more cost-effectively in the nursing home setting than in the general hospital, a major drawback to using the nursing home as a place for dying is that often insurance does not cover the cost of the nursing home care (just as it often does not cover the cost of care at home). Currently, there is almost no private insurance for nursing home care, and Medicare now covers only about 3 percent of nursing home days. The rest must be covered by a combination of Medicaid, to be eligible for which a patient must be pauperized, and private pay. It is essential that federal and private health care plans be modified to make nursing home care more accessible to patients of limited means.*

Hospital

As much as one third of the patients cared for at home and expected to die there actually die in the hospital, even when hospice techniques of home care are used. The symptoms or anxiety generated by an impending death may overwhelm the family, and recourse to the hospital is appropriate whenever any treatment program, including a psychosocial one, cannot palliate the distress felt by the patient, the family, or both.

To accommodate such families and patients, hospitals should consider the development of specialized units, with rooms appointed so as to provide pleasant surroundings that will facilitate comfortable interchange among patient, family, and friends. The presence of life-sustaining equipment would be inappropriate in such an environment.

The intensive care unit should generally be discouraged as a treatment setting for the hospitalized patient who is dying, unless intensive palliative measures are required that cannot be done elsewhere. Too often, life-sustaining measures are instituted in the intensive care unit

---

*The Catastrophic Health Care Act of 1989 increased the Medicare contribution to care in a Skilled Nursing Facility by approximately one-third.—Eds.

without sufficient thought to the proper goals of treatment. Although the courts have held that in the treatment of the hopelessly ill there is no legal distinction between stopping treatment and not starting it in the first place, there is a bias in the intensive care unit toward continuing aggressive measures that may be inappropriate. Though difficult, it is possible for a patient to die in the intensive care unit with dignity and comfort, since medical hardware itself has no capacity to dehumanize anyone. The important point is that the physician set a tone of caring and support, no matter what the setting.

Although the physicians and nurses in intensive care units may be less prepared than other professionals to switch from aggressive curative care to palliation and the provision of comfort only, they have all seen many situations in which clear decisions to limit treatment have brought welcome relief. Since these caregivers often have considerable emotional energy invested in patients who have previously been receiving aggressive curative treatment, they may need consultation with colleagues from outside the intensive care unit to decide when to change the treatment goals.

TREATING THE DYING PATIENT: THE IMPORTANCE OF FLEXIBLE CARE

The care of the dying is an art that should have its fullest expression in helping patients cope with the technologically complicated medical environment that often surrounds them at the end of life. The concept of a good death does not mean simply the withholding of technological treatments that serve only to prolong the act of dying. It also requires the art of deliberately creating a medical environment that allows a peaceful death. Somewhere between the unacceptable extremes of failure to treat the dying patient and intolerable use of aggressive life-sustaining measures, the physician must seek a level of care that optimizes comfort and dignity.

In evaluating the burdens and benefits of treatment for the dying patient—whether in the hospital, in a nursing home, or at home—the physician needs to formulate a flexible and adjustable care plan, tailoring the treatment to the patient's changing needs as the disease progresses. Such plans contrast sharply with the practice, frequent in medicine, in which the physician makes rounds and prescribes, leaving orders for nurses and technicians, but not giving continual feedback and adjustment. The physician's actions on behalf of the patient should be appropriate, with respect to both the types of treatments and the location in which they are given. Such actions need to be adjusted continually to the individual patient's needs, with the physician keeping primarily in mind that the benefits of treatment must outweigh the burdens imposed.

When the patient lacks decision-making capacity, discussing the limitation of treatment with the family becomes a major part of the treatment plan. The principle of continually adjusted care should guide all these decisions.

Pain and Suffering

The principle of continually adjusted care is nowhere more important than in the control of pain, fear, and suffering. The hopelessly ill patient must have whatever is necessary to control pain. One of the most pervasive causes of anxiety among patients, their families, and the public is the perception that physicians' efforts toward the relief of pain are sadly deficient. Because of this perceived professional deficiency, people fear that needless suffering will be allowed to occur as patients are dying.[18] To a large extent, we believe such fears are justified.

In the patient whose dying process is irreversible, the balance between minimizing pain and suffering and potentially hastening death should be struck clearly in favor of pain relief. Narcotics or other pain medications should be given in whatever dose and by whatever route is necessary for relief. It is morally correct to increase the dose of narcotics to whatever dose is needed, even though the medication may contribute to the depression of respiration or blood pressure, the dulling of consciousness, or even death, provided the primary goal of the physician is to relieve suffering. The proper dose of pain medication is the dose that is sufficient to relieve pain and suffering, even to the point of unconsciousness.

Dying patients often feel isolated and doubt seriously that their physician will be there to relieve their pain when the terminal phase is near. Early in the course of fatal disease, patients should be offered strong reassurance that pain will be controlled and that their physician will be available when the need is greatest. Both the patient and the family should be told that addiction need not be a source of concern and that the relief of pain will have nothing but a salutary effect from both the physical and the emotional standpoint. When possible, pain medication should be given orally to maximize patient autonomy, but usually a continuous parenteral route is needed for the adequate medication of patients in the near-terminal or terminal state. Under no circumstances should medication be "rationed." For episodic pain, patients should be encouraged to take medication as soon as they are conscious of pain, instead of waiting until it becomes intense and far more difficult to control. For continuous or frequently recurring pain, the patient should be placed on a regular schedule of administration. Some patients will choose to endure a degree of pain rather than experience any loss of alertness or control from taking narcotics— a choice that is consistent with patient autonomy and the concept of continually adjusted care.

If pain cannot be controlled with the commonly used analgesic regimens of mild or moderate strength, the patient should be switched quickly to more potent narcotics. It is important that doses be adequate: the textbook doses recommended for short-term pain are often grossly inadequate for long-term pain in the patient dying of cancer. The physician should be familiar with two or three narcotics and their side effects and appropriate starting dosages. Doses should be brought promptly to levels that provide a reliable pain-free state. Since adequate narcotic management seems to be an unfamiliar area to many physicians, we urge that educational material be distributed to them from a noncommercial source.[19] To allow a patient to experience unbearable pain or suffering is unethical medical practice.

Legal Concerns

The principles of medical ethics are formulated independently of legal decisions, but physicians may fear that decisions about the care of the hopelessly ill will bring special risks of criminal charges and prosecution. Although no medical decision can be immune from legal scrutiny, courts in the United States have generally supported the approaches advocated here.[20-23] The physician should follow these principles without exaggerated concern for legal consequences, doing whatever is necessary to relieve pain and bring comfort, and adhering to the patient's wishes as much as possible. To withhold any necessary measure of pain relief in a hopelessly ill person out of fear of depressing respiration or of possible legal repercussions is unjustifiable. Good medical practice is the best protection against legal liability.

Preparing for Death

As sickness progesses toward death, measures to minimize suffering should be intensified. Dying patients may require palliative care of an intensity that rivals even that of curative efforts. Keeping the patient clean, caring for the skin, preventing the formation of bed sores, treating neuropsychiatric symptoms, controlling peripheral and pulmonary edema, aggressively reducing nausea and vomiting, using intravenous medications, fighting the psychosocial forces that can lead to family fragmentation—all can tax the ingenuity and equanimity of the most skilled health professionals. Even though aggressive curative techniques are no longer indicated, professionals and families are still called on to use intensive measures—extreme responsibility, extraordinary sensitivity, and heroic compassion.

In training programs for physicians, more attention needs to be paid to these aspects of care. Progress has been made in persuading house staff and attending physicians to discuss DNR orders and to include clear orders and notes in the chart about limits on life-sustaining therapies, but patients are too rarely cared for directly by the physician at or near the time of death. Usually it is nurses who care for patients at this time. In a few innovative training programs, most notably at the University of Oregon, the hands-on aspects of care of the dying are addressed,[24] and such techniques should be presented at all training institutions.

ASSISTED SUICIDE

If care is administered properly at the end of life, only the rare patient should be so distressed that he or she desires to commit suicide. Occasionally, however, all fails. The doctor, the nurse, the family, and the patient may have done everything possible to relieve the distress occasioned by a terminal illness, and yet the patient perceives his or her situation as intolerable and seeks assistance in bringing about death. Is it ever justifiable for the physician to assist suicide in such a case?

Some physicians, believing it to be the last act in a continuum of care provided for the hopelessly ill patient, do assist patients who request it, either by prescribing sleeping pills with knowledge of their intended use or by discussing the required doses and methods of administration with the patient. The frequency with which such actions are undertaken is unknown, but they are certainly not rare. Suicide differs from euthanasia in that the act of bringing on death is performed by the patient, not the physician.

The physician who considers helping a patient who requests assistance with suicide must determine first that the patient is indeed beyond all help and not merely suffering from a treatable depression of the sort common in people with terminal illnesses. Such a depression requires therapeutic intervention. If there is no treatable component to the depression and the patient's pain or suffering is refractory to treatment, then the wish for suicide may be rational. If such a patient acts on the wish for death and actually commits suicide, it is ethical for a physician who knows the patient to refrain from an attempt at resuscitation.

Even though suicide itself is not illegal, helping a person commit suicide is a crime in many states, either by statute or under common law. Even so, we know of no physician who has ever been prosecuted in the United States for prescribing sleeping pills in order to help a patient commit suicide.[25] However, the potential illegality of this act is a deterrent, and apart from that, some physicians simply cannot bring themselves to assist in suicide or to condone such action.

Whether it is bad medical practice or immoral to help a hopelessly ill patient commit a rational suicide is a complex issue, provoking a number of considerations. First, as their disease advances, patients may lose their decision-making capacity because of the effects of the disease or the drug treatment. Assisting such patients with suicide comes close to performing an act of euthanasia. Second, patients who want a doctor's assistance with suicide may be unwilling to endure their terminal illness because they lack information about what is ahead. Even when the physician explains in careful detail the availability of the kind of flexible, continually adjusted care described here, the patient may still opt out of that treatment plan and reject the physician's efforts to ease the dying process. Also, what are the physician's obligations if a patient who retains decision-making capacity insists that family members not be told of a suicide plan?

Should the physician insist on obtaining the family's consent? Finally, should physicians acknowledge their role in the suicide in some way—by obtaining consultation, or in writing? Physicians who act in secret become isolated and cannot consult colleagues or ethics committees for confirmation that the patient has made a rational decision. If contacted, such colleagues may well object and even consider themselves obliged to report the physician to the Board of Medical Licensure or to the prosecutor. The impulse to maintain secrecy gives the lie to the moral intuition that assistance with suicide is ethical.

It is difficult to answer such questions, but all but two of us (J. v. E. and E. H. C.) believe that it is not immoral for a physician to assist in the rational suicide of a terminally ill person. However, we recognize that such an act represents a departure from the principle of continually adjusted care that we have presented. As such, it should be considered a separate alternative and not an extension of the flexible approach to care that we have recommended. Clearly, the subject of assisted suicide deserves wide and open discussion.

EUTHANASIA

Some patients who cannot carry out suicide plans themselves, with or without assistance, may ask their physicians to take a more active part in ending their lives. In the case of suicide, the final act is performed by the patient, even when the physician provides indirect assistance in the form of information and means. By contrast, euthanasia requires the physician to perform a medical procedure that causes death directly. It is therefore even more controversial than assisted rational suicide, and various arguments have been mustered through the years for and against its use.[26,27]

In the Netherlands, the practice of euthanasia has gained a degree of social acceptance. As a result of a 1984 decision by the Dutch Supreme Court, euthanasia is no longer prosecuted in certain approved circumstances. The Dutch government authorized the State Commission on Euthanasia to study the issue, and the commission's report favored permitting doctors to perform euthanasia with certain safeguards, but the Dutch parliament, the States-General, has not yet acted to change the law.

Many Dutch physicians believe, however, that the medical treatments and actions needed to keep dying patients comfortable may at times be extended to include the act of euthanasia. Some of them hold that a continuum of measures can be brought into play to help the patient, and occasionally the injection of a lethal dose of a drug (usually a short-acting barbiturate, followed by a paralyzing agent) becomes necessary, representing the extreme end of that continuum. This occurs between 5,000 and 10,000 times a year in the Netherlands, according to van der Werf[28] (and P. Admiraal: personal communication).

The medical community in the Netherlands has developed criteria that must be met for an act of euthanasia to be considered medically and ethically acceptable.[29] The patient's medical situation must be intolerable, with no prospect of improvement. The patient must be rational and must voluntarily and repeatedly request euthanasia of the physician. The patient must be fully informed. There must be no other means of relieving the suffering, and two physicians must concur with the request.

In recent years, euthanasia has been discussed more openly in the United States, and the public response has been increasingly favorable. When a Roper poll asked in 1988 whether a physician should be lawfully able to end the life of a terminally ill patient at the patient's request, 58 percent said yes, 27 percent said no, and 10 percent were undecided. (This poll, taken for the National Hemlock Society by the Roper Organization of New York City, surveyed 1,982 adult Americans in March 1988.)

Presumably, the majority of physicians in the United States do not favor the Dutch position. Many physicians oppose euthanasia on moral or religious grounds, and indeed it raises profound theological questions. All religions address the matter of whether it is proper to decide the time of one's death. Whatever attitudes society may develop toward assisted suicide or euthanasia, individual physicians should not feel morally coerced to participate in such approaches. Many physicians oppose euthanasia because they believe it to be outside the physician's role, and some fear that it may be subject to abuse. (Some physicians and laypersons fear that active voluntary euthanasia, as practiced in the Netherlands, could lead to involuntary euthanasia and to murder, as practiced by the Nazis. Ethically, however, the difference is obvious.) In addition, the social climate in this country is very litigious, and the likelihood of prosecution if a case of euthanasia were discovered is fairly high—much higher than the likelihood of prosecution after a suicide in which the physician has assisted. Thus, the prospect of criminal prosecution deters even the hardiest advocates of euthanasia among physicians.

Nevertheless, the medical profession and the public will continue to debate the role that euthanasia may have in the treatment of the terminally or hopelessly ill patient.

NOTES

1. S. H. Wanzer, S. J. Adelstein, R. E. Cranford, et al. "The Physician's Responsibility toward Hopelessly Ill Patients. *The New England Journal of Medicine* 310 (1984): 955-959.

2. President's Commission for the Study of Ethical Problems in Medicine and Biomedical and Behavioral Research. *Deciding to Forego Life-Sustaining Treatment: A Report on the Ethical, Medical, and Legal Issues in Treatment Decisions* (Washington, D.C.: Government Printing Office, 1983).

3. Office of Technology Assessment. *Life-Sustaining Technologies and the Elderly* (Washington, D.C.: Government Printing Office, 1987).

4. Senate Special Committee on Aging. *A Matter of Choice: Planning Ahead for Health Care Decisions* (Washington, D.C.: Government Printing Office, 1987).

5. *Guidelines on the Termination of Life-Sustaining Treatment and the Care of the Dying: A Report by the Hastings Center* (Briarcliff Manor, N.Y.: Hastings Center, 1987).

6. Current Opinions of the Council on Ethical and Judicial Affairs of the American Medical Association—1986. *Withholding or Withdrawing Life-Prolonging Treatment* (Chicago: American Medical Association, 1986).

7. Executive Board of the American Academy of Neurology. *Position of the American Academy of Neurology on Certain Aspects of the Care and Management of the Persistent Vegetative State Patient* (Minneapolis: American Academy of Neurology, 1988).

8. J. E. Ruark and T. A. Raffin, Stanford University Medical Center Committee on Ethics. "Initiating and Withdrawing Life Support." *The New England Journal of Medicine* 381 (1988): 25-30.

9. P. Safar and N. Bircher, *Cardiopulmonary Cerebral Resuscitation: An Introduction to Resuscitation Medicine.* 3rd ed. (Philadelphia: W. B. Saunders, 1988).

10. Society for the Right to Die, *Handbook of Living Will Laws.* (New York: Society for the Right to Die, 1987).

11. *Appointing a Proxy for Health Care Decisions* (New York: Society for the Right to Die, 1988).

12. *Adult Right to Die Case Citations* (New York: Society for the Right to Die, 1988).

13. *Right to Die Court Decisions: Artificial Feeding* (New York: Society for the Right to Die, 1988).

14. Associated Press Media General, Poll no. 4, Richmond, Va.: Media General (February 1985).

15. California Department of Health Services, *Guidelines Regarding Withdrawal or Withholding of Life-Sustaining Procedure(s) in Long-Term Care Facilities* (August 7, 1987).

16. S. E. Bedell, D. Pelle, P. L. Maher, and P. D. Cleary, "Do-Not-Resuscitate Orders for Critically Ill Patients in the Hospital: How Are They Used and What Is Their Impact?" *Journal of the American Medical Association* 256 (1986): 233-237.

17. W. Bulkin, and·H. Lukashok, "Rx for Dying: The Case for Hospice." *The New England Journal of Medicine* 318 (1988): 376-378.

18. M. Angell, "The Quality of Mercy," *The New England Journal of Medicine* 306 (1982): 98-99.

19. R. Payne and K. M. Foley, eds. "Cancer Pain." *Medical Clinician of North America* 71 (1987): 153-352.

20. *Bartling* v. *Superior Court* (Glendale Adventist Medical Center), 163 Cal. App. 3d 186. 209 Rptr. 220 (Ct. App. 1984).

21. *Bouvia* v. *Superior Court* (Glenchur). 179 Cal. App. 3d 1127. 225 Cal. Rptr. 297 (Ct. App. 1986). review denied (Cal. June 5, 1986).

22. *Brophy* v. *New England Sinai Hosp., Inc.,* 398 Mass. 417. 497. N.E. 2d 626 (1986).

23. In re Culham. No. 87-340537-AC (Mich. Cir. Ct., Oakland County, Dec. 15, 1987) (J. Breck).

24. S. W. Tolle, D. H. Hickham, E. B. Larson, and J. A. Benson, "Patient Death and House-Staff Stress," *Clinical Research* 35 (1987): 762A, abstract.

25. L. H. Glanz, "Withholding and Withdrawing Treatment: The Role of the Criminal Law," *Law, Medicine, and Health Care* 15 (1987-1988): 231-241.

26. H. Van Bommel, *Choices for People Who Have a Terminal Illness, Their Families and Their Caregivers* (Toronto: N. C. Press, 1986).

27. M. Angell, "Euthanasia," *The New England Journal of Medicine* 319 (1988): 1348-1350.

28. G. T. van der Wert, "Huisarts en euthanasie." *Medisch Contact* 43 (1986): 1389.

29. The Central Committee of the Royal Dutch Medical Association. *Vision on Euthanasia* (Utrecht: Netherlands, 1986).

20

Missouri v. Cruzan

Chief Justice Rehnquist delivered the opinion of the Court, in which Justices White, O'Connor, Scalia, and Kennedy joined. Justices O'Connor and Scalia filed concurring opinions. Justice Brennan filed a dissenting opinion, in which Justices Marshall and Blackmun joined. Justice Stevens filed a dissenting opinion.

Petitioner Nancy Beth Cruzan was rendered incompetent as a result of severe injuries sustained during an automobile accident. Co-petitioners Lester and Joyce Cruzan, Nancy's parents and co-guardians, sought a court order directing the withdrawal of their daughter's artificial feeding and hydration equipment after it became apparent that she had virtually no chance of recovering her cognitive faculties. The Supreme Court of Missouri held that because there was no clear and convincing evidence of Nancy's desire to have life-sustaining treatment withdrawn under such circumstances, her parents lacked authority to effectuate such a request. We granted certiorari, and now affirm.

On the night of January 11, 1983, Nancy Cruzan lost control of her car as she traveled down Elm Road in Jasper County, Missouri. The vehicle overturned, and Cruzan was discovered lying face down in a ditch without detectable respiratory or cardiac function. Paramedics were able to restore her breathing and heartbeat at the accident site, and she was transported to a hospital in an unconscious state. An attending neurosurgeon diagnosed her as having sustained probable

179

cerebral contusions compounded by significant anoxia (lack of oxygen). The Missouri trial court in this case found that permanent brain damage generally results after six minutes in an anoxic state; it was estimated that Cruzan was deprived of oxygen from twelve to fourteen minutes. She remained in a coma for approximately three weeks and then progressed to an unconscious state in which she was able to orally ingest some nutrition. In order to ease feeding and further the recovery, surgeons implanted a gastrostomy feeding and hydration tube in Cruzan with the consent of her then husband. Subsequent rehabilitative efforts proved unavailing. She now lies in a Missouri state hospital in what is commonly referred to as a persistent vegetative state: generally, a condition in which a person exhibits motor reflexes but evinces no indications of significant cognitive function.[1] The State of Missouri is bearing the cost of her care.

After it became apparent that Nancy Cruzan had virtually no chance of regaining her mental faculties her parents asked hospital employees to terminate the artificial nutrition and hydration procedures. All agree that such a removal would cause her death. The employees refused to honor the request without court approval. The

---

1. The State Supreme Court, adopting much of the trial court's findings, described Nancy Cruzan's medical condition as follows:

". . . (1) [H]er respiration and circulation are not artificially maintained and are within the normal limits of a thirty-year-old female; (2) she is oblivious to her environment except for reflexive responses to sound and perhaps painful stimuli; (3) she suffered anoxia of the brain resulting in a massive enlargement of the ventricles filling with cerebrospinal fluid in the area where the brain has degenerated and [her] cerebral cortical atrophy is irreversible, permanent, progressive and ongoing; (4) her highest cognitive brain function is exhibited by her grimacing, perhaps in recognition of ordinary painful stimuli, indicating the experience of pain and apparent response to sound; (5) she is a spastic quadriplegic; (6) her four extremities are contracted with irreversible muscular and tendon damage to all extremities; (7) she has no cognitive or reflexive ability to swallow food or water to maintain her daily essential needs and . . . she will never recover her ability to swallow sufficient [sic] to satisfy her needs. In sum, Nancy is diagnosed as in a persistent vegetative state. She is not dead. She is not terminally ill. Medical experts testified that she could live another thirty years" [*Cruzan* v. *Harmon* (Mo. 1989].

In observing that Cruzan was not dead, the court referred to the following Missouri statute:
"For all legal purposes, the occurrence of human death shall be determined in accordance with the usual and customary standards of medical practice, provided that death shall not be determined to have occurred unless the following minimal conditions have been met:

"(1) When respiration and circulation are not artificially maintained, there is an irreversible cessation of spontaneous respiration and circulation; or

"(2) When respiration and circulation are artificially maintained, and there is total and irreversible cessation of all brain function, including the brain stem and that such determination is made by a licensed physician." [Mo. Rev. Stat. @ 194.005 (1986)]

Since Cruzan's respiration and circulation were not being artificially maintained, she obviously fit within the first proviso of the statute.

parents then sought and received authorization from the state trial court for termination. The court found that a person in Nancy's condition had a fundamental right under the State and Federal Constitutions to refuse or direct the withdrawal of "death prolonging procedures." The court also found that Nancy's "expressed thoughts at age twenty-five in somewhat serious conversation with a housemate friend that if sick or injured she would not wish to continue her life unless she could live at least halfway normally suggests that given her present condition she would not wish to continue on with her nutrition and hydration."

The Supreme Court of Missouri reversed by a divided vote. The court recognized a right to refuse treatment embodied in the common-law doctrine of informed consent, but expressed skepticism about the application of that doctrine in the circumstances of this case. The court also declined to read a broad right of privacy into the State Constitution which would "support the right of a person to refuse medical treatment in every circumstance," and expressed doubt as to whether such a right existed under the United States Constitution. It then decided that the Missouri Living Will statute embodied a state policy strongly favoring the preservation of life. The court found that Cruzan's statements to her roommate regarding her desire to live or die under certain conditions were "unreliable for the purpose of determining her intent, and thus insufficient to support the co-guardians claim to exercise substituted judgment on Nancy's behalf." It rejected the argument that Cruzan's parents were entitled to order the termination of her medical treatment, concluding that "no person can assume that choice for an incompetent in the absence of the formalities required under Missouri's Living Will statutes or the clear and convincing, inherently reliable evidence absent here." The court also expressed its view that "[b]road policy questions bearing on life and death are more properly addressed by representative assemblies" than judicial bodies.

We granted certiorari to consider the question of whether Cruzan has a right under the United States Constitution which would require the hospital to withdraw life-sustaining treatment from her under these circumstances.

At common law, even the touching of one person by another without consent and without legal justification was a battery. Before the turn of the century, this Court observed that "[n]o right is held more sacred, or is more carefully guarded, by the common law, than the right of every individual to the possession and control of his own person, free from all restraint or interference of others, unless by clear and unquestionable authority of law" *Union Pacific R. Co.* v. *Botsford* (1891). This notion of bodily integrity has been embodied in the requirement that informed consent is generally required for medical treatment. Justice Cardozo, while on the Court of Appeals of New York, aptly described this doctrine: "Every human being of adult years and sound mind has a right to determine what shall be done with his own body; and a surgeon who performs an operation without his patient's consent commits an assault, for which he is liable in damages" *Schloendorff* v. *Society of New York Hospital* (1914). The informed consent doctrine has become firmly entrenched in American tort law.

The logical corollary of the doctrine of informed consent is that the patient generally possesses the right not to consent, that is, to refuse treatment. Until about fifteen years ago and the seminal decision in *In re Quinlan,* . . . the number of right-to-refuse-treatment decisions were relatively few. Most of the earlier cases involved patients who refused medical treatment forbidden by their religious beliefs, thus implicating First Amendment rights as well as common-law rights of self-determination. More recently, however, with the advance of medical technology capable of sustaining life well past the point where natural forces would have brought certain death in earlier times, cases involving the right to refuse life-sustaining treatment have burgeoned.

In the Quinlan case, young Karen Quinlan suffered severe brain damage as the result of anoxia, and entered a persistent vegetative state. Karen's father sought judicial approval to disconnect his daughter's respirator. The New Jersey Supreme Court granted the relief, holding that Karen had a right of privacy grounded in the Federal Constitution to terminate treatment. Recognizing that this right was not absolute, however, the court balanced it against asserted state interests. Noting that the State's interest "weakens and the individual's right to privacy grows as the degree of bodily invasion increases and the prognosis dims," the court concluded that the state interests had to give way in that case. The court also concluded that the "only practical way" to prevent the loss of Karen's privacy right due to her incompetence was to allow her guardian and family to decide "whether she would exercise it in these circumstances."

After *Quinlan,* however, most courts have based a right to refuse treatment either solely on the common-law right to informed consent or on both the common-law right and a constitutional privacy right. . . .

As [many state court] cases demonstrate, the common-law doctrine of informed consent is viewed as generally encompassing the right of a competent individual to refuse medical treatment. Beyond that, these decisions demonstrate both similarity and diversity in their approach to decision of what all agree is a perplexing question with unusually strong moral and ethical overtones. State courts have available to them for decision a number of sources—state constitutions, statutes, and common law—which are not available to us. In this Court, the question is simply and starkly whether the United States Constitution prohibits Missouri from choosing the rule of decision which it did. This is the first case in which we have been squarely presented with the issue of whether the United States Constitution grants what is in common parlance referred to as a "right to die." We follow the judicious counsel of our decision in *Twin City Bank* v. *Nebeker* (1897), where we said that in deciding "a question of such magnitude and importance . . . it is the [better] part of wisdom not to attempt, by any general statement, to cover every possible phase of the subject."

The Fourteenth Amendment provides that no State shall "deprive any person of life, liberty, or property, without due process of law." The principle that a competent person has a constitutionally protected liberty interest in refusing unwanted medical treatment may be inferred from our prior decisions. . . .

But determining that a person has a "liberty interest" under the Due Process Clause does not end the inquiry;[2] "whether respondent's constitutional rights have been violated must be determined by balancing his liberty interests against the relevant state interests" *Youngberg* v. *Romeo* (1982).

Petitioners insist that under the general holdings of our cases, the forced administration of life-sustaining medical treatment, and even of artificially-delivered food and water essential to life, would implicate a competent person's liberty interest. Although we think

---

2. Although many state courts have held that a right to refuse treatment is encompassed by a generalized constitutional right of privacy, we have never so held. We believe this issue is more properly analyzed in terms of a Fourteenth Amendment liberty interest.

the logic of the cases discussed above would embrace such a liberty interest, the dramatic consequences involved in refusal of such treatment would inform the inquiry as to whether the deprivation of that interest is constitutionally permissible. But for purposes of this case, we assume that the United States Constitution would grant a competent person a constitutionally protected right to refuse lifesaving hydration and nutrition.

Petitioners go on to assert that an incompetent person should possess the same right in this respect as is possessed by a competent person. . . .

The difficulty with petitioners' claim is that in a sense it begs the question: an incompetent person is not able to make an informed and voluntary choice to exercise a hypothetical right to refuse treatment or any other right. Such a "right" must be exercised for her, if at all, by some sort of surrogate. Here, Missouri has in effect recognized that under certain circumstances a surrogate may act for the patient in electing to have hydration and nutrition withdrawn in such a way as to cause death, but it has established a procedural safeguard to assure that the action of the surrogate conforms as best it may to the wishes expressed by the patient while competent. Missouri requires that evidence of the incompetent's wishes as to the withdrawal of treatment be proved by clear and convincing evidence. The question, then, is whether the United States Constitution forbids the establishment of this procedural requirement by the State. We hold that it does not.

Whether or not Missouri's clear and convincing evidence requirement comports with the United States Constitution depends in part on what interests the State may properly seek to protect in this situation. Missouri relies on its interest in the protection and preservation of human life, and there can be no gainsaying this interest. As a general matter, the States—indeed, all civilized nations—demonstrate their commitment to life by treating homicide as serious crime. Moreover, the majority of States in this country have laws imposing criminal penalties on one who assists another to commit suicide. We do not think a State is required to remain neutral in the face of an informed and voluntary decision by a physically-able adult to starve to death.

But in the context presented here, a State has more particular interests at stake. The choice between life and death is a deeply personal decision of obvious and overwhelming finality. We believe Missouri may legitimately seek to safeguard the personal element of this choice through the imposition of heightened evidentiary requirements. It cannot be disputed that the Due Process Clause protects an interest in life as well as an interest in refusing life-sustaining medical treatment. Not all incompetent patients will have loved ones available to serve as surrogate decisionmakers. And even where family members are present, "[t]here will, of course, be some unfortunate situations in which family members will not act to protect a patient" *In re Jobes* (1987). A State is entitled to guard against potential abuses in such situations. Similarly, a State is entitled to consider that a judicial proceeding to make a determination regarding an incompetent's wishes may very well not be an adversarial one, with the added guarantee of accurate factfinding that the adversary process brings with it. Finally, we think a State may properly decline to make judgments about the "quality" of life that a particular individual may enjoy, and simply assert an unqualified interest in the preservation of human life to be weighed against the constitutionally protected interests of the individual.

In our view, Missouri has permissibly sought to advance these interests through the adoption of a "clear and convincing" standard of proof to govern such proceedings. "The function of a standard of proof, as that concept is embodied in the Due Process Clause and in the realm of factfinding, is to 'instruct the factfinder concerning the degree of confidence our society thinks he should have in the correctness of factual conclusions for a particular type of adjudication' " *Addington* v. *Texas* (1979).

We think it self-evident that the interests at stake in the instant proceedings are more substantial, both on an individual and societal level, than those involved in a run-of-the-mine civil dispute. But not only does the standard of proof reflect the importance of a particular adjudication, it also serves as "a societal judgment about how the risk of error should be distributed betwen the litigants" *Santosky* v. *Kramer* (1982). The more stringent the burden of proof a party must bear, the more that party bears the risk of an erroneous decision. We believe that Missouri may permissibly place an increased risk of an erroneous decision on those seeking to terminate an incompetent individual's life-sustaining treatment. An erroneous decision not to terminate results in a maintenance of the status quo; the possibility of subsequent developments such as advancements in medical science, the discovery of new evidence regarding the patient's intent, changes in the law, or simply the unexpected death of the patient despite the administration of life-sustaining treatment, at least create the potential that a wrong decision will eventually be corrected or its impact mitigated. An erroneous decision to withdraw life-sustaining treatment, however, is not susceptible of correction. . . .

. . . There is no doubt that statutes requiring wills to be in writing, and statutes of frauds which require that a contract to make a will be in writing, on occasion frustrate the effectuation of the not-fully-expressed desires of Nancy Cruzan. But the Constitution does not require general rules to work faultlessly; no general rule can.

In sum, we conclude that a State may apply a clear and convincing evidence standard in proceedings where a guardian seeks to discontinue nutrition and hydration of a person diagnosed to be in a persistent vegetative state. We note that many courts which have adopted some sort of substituted judgment procedure in situations like this, whether they limit consideration of evidence to the prior expressed wishes of the incompetent individual, or whether they allow more general proof of what the individual's decision would have been, require a clear and convincing standard of proof for such evidence.

The Supreme Court of Missouri held that in this case the testimony adduced at trial did not amount to clear and convincing proof of the patient's desire to have hydration and nutrition withdrawn. In so doing, it reversed a decision of the Missouri trial court which had found that the evidence "suggest[ed]" Nancy Cruzan would not have desired to continue such measures, but which had not adopted the standard of "clear and convincing evidence" enunciated by the Supreme Court. The testimony adduced at trial consisted primarily of Nancy Cruzan's statements made to a housemate about a year before her accident that she would not want to live should she face life as a "vegetable," and other observations to the same effect. The observations did not deal in terms with withdrawal of medical treatment or of hydration and nutrition. We cannot say that the Supreme Court of Missouri committed constitutional error in reaching the conclusion that it did.

Petitioners alternatively contend that Missouri must accept the "judgment" of close family members even in the absence of substantial proof that their views reflect the views of the patient. They rely primarily upon our decisions in *Michael H.* v. *Gerald D.* (1989), and *Parham* v. *J. R.* (1979). But we do not think these cases support their claim. In *Michael H.,* we upheld the constitutionality of California's favored treatment of traditional family relationships; such a holding may not be turned around into a constitutional requirement that a State must recognize the primacy of those relationships in a situation like this. And in *Parham,* where the patient was a minor, we also upheld the constitutionality of a state scheme in which parents made certain decisions for mentally ill minors. Here again petitioners would seek to turn a decision which allowed a State to rely on family decision making into a constitutional requirement that the State recognize such decision making. But constitutional law does not work that way.

No doubt is engendered by anything in this record but that Nancy Cruzan's mother and father are loving and caring parents. If the State were required by the United States Constitution to repose a right of "substituted judgment" with anyone, the Cruzans would surely qualify. But we do not think the Due Process Clause requires the State to repose judgment on these matters with anyone but the patient herself. Close family members may have a strong feeling—a feeling not at all ignoble or unworthy, but not entirely disinterested, either—that they do not wish to witness the continuation of the life of a loved one which they regard as hopeless, meaningless, and even degrading. But there is no automatic assurance that the view of close family members will necessarily be the same as the patient's would have been had she been confronted with the prospect of her situation while competent. All of the reasons previously discussed for allowing Missouri to require clear and convincing evidence of the patient's wishes lead us to conclude that the State may choose to defer only to those wishes, rather than confide the decision to close family members.[3]

The judgment of the Supreme Court of Missouri is Affirmed.

---

3. We are not faced in this case with the question of whether a State might be required to defer to the decision of a surrogate if competent and probative evidence established that the patient herself had expressed a desire that the decision to terminate life-sustaining treatment be made for her by that individual.

Petitioners also adumbrate in their brief a claim based on the Equal Protection Clause of the Fourteenth Amendment to the effect that Missouri has impermissibly treated incompetent patients differently from competent ones, citing the statement in *Cleburne* v. *Cleburne Living Center, Inc.* (1985), that the clause is "essentially a direction that all persons similarly situated should be treated alike." The differences between the choice made by a competent person to refuse medical treatment, and the choice made for an incompetent person by someone else to refuse medical treatment, are so obviously different that the State is warranted in establishing rigorous procedures for the latter class of cases which do not apply to the former class.

JUSTICE O'CONNOR, concurring. . . .

Today's decision, holding only that the Constitution permits a State to require clear and convincing evidence of Nancy Cruzan's desire to have artificial hydration and nutrition withdrawn, does not preclude a future determination that the Constitution requires the States to implement the decisions of a patient's duly appointed surrogate. Nor does it prevent States from developing other approaches for protecting an incompetent individual's liberty interest in refusing medical treatment. As is evident from the Court's survey of state court decisions, no national consensus has yet emerged on the best solution for this difficult and sensitive problem. Today we decide only that one State's practice does not violate the Constitution; the more challenging task of crafting appropriate procedures for safeguarding incompetents' liberty interests is entrusted to the "laboratory" of the States in the first instance.

JUSTICE SCALIA, concurring. . . .

The various opinions in this case portray quite clearly the difficult, indeed agonizing, questions that are presented by the constantly increasing power of science to keep the human body alive for longer than any reasonable person would want to inhabit it. The States have begun to grapple with these problems through legislation. I am concerned, from the tenor of today's opinions, that we are poised to confuse that enterprise as successfully as we have confused the enterprise of legislating concerning abortion—requiring it to be conducted against a background of federal constitutional imperatives that are unknown because they are being newly crafted from Term to Term. That would be a great misfortune.

While I agree with the Court's analysis today, and therefore join in its opinion, I would have preferred that we announce, clearly and promptly, that the federal courts have no business in this field; that American law has always accorded the State the power to prevent, by force if necessary, suicide—including suicide by refusing to take appropriate measures necessary to preserve one's life; that the point at which life becomes "worthless," and the point at which the means necessary to preserve it become "extraordinary" or "inappropriate," are neither set forth in the Constitution nor known to the nine Justices of this Court any better than they are known to nine people picked at random from the Kansas City telephone directory; and hence, that even when it is demonstrated by clear and convincing evidence that a patient no longer wishes certain measures to be taken to preserve her life, it is up to the citizens of Missouri to decide, through their elected representatives, whether that wish will be honored. It is quite impossible (because the Constitution says nothing about the matter) that those citizens will decide upon a line less lawful than the one we would choose; and it is unlikely (because we know no more about "life-and-death" than they do) that they will decide upon a line less reasonable.

*   *   *

Petitioners rely on three distinctions to separate Nancy Cruzan's case from ordinary suicide: (1) that she is permanently incapacitated and in pain; (2) that she would bring on her death not by any affirmative act but by merely declining treatment that provides nourishment; and (3) that preventing her from effectuating her presumed wish to die requires violation of her bodily integrity. None of these suffices. Suicide was not excused even when committed "to avoid those ills which [persons] had not the fortitude to endure" (4 W. *Blackstone Commentaries*). "The life of those to whom life has become a burden—of those who are hopelessly diseased or fatally wounded—nay, even the lives of criminals condemned to death, are under the protection of the law, equally as the lives of those who are in the full tide of life's enjoyment, and anxious to continue to live" *Blackburn* v. *State* (1873). Thus, a man who prepared a poison, and placed it within reach of his wife, "to put an end to her suffering" from a terminal illness was convicted of murder (*People* v. *Roberts* [1920]); the "incurable suffering of the suicide, as a legal question, could hardly affect the degree of criminality . . ." (*Yale Law Journal* [1921]). Nor would the imminence of the patient's death have affected liability. "The lives of all are equally under the protection of the law, and under that protection to their last moment. . . . [Assisted suicide] is declared by the law to be murder, irrespective of the wishes or the condition of the party to whom the poison is administered . . ." *Blackburn.*

The second asserted distinction—suggested by the recent cases

canvassed by the Court concerning the right to refuse treatment—
relies on the dichotomy between action and inaction. Suicide, it is
said, consists of an affirmative act to end one's life; refusing treatment is not an affirmative act "causing" death, but merely a passive
acceptance of the natural process of dying. I readily acknowledge
that the distinction between action and inaction has some bearing
upon the legislative judgment of what ought to be prevented as suicide—though even there it would seem to me unreasonable to draw
the line precisely between action and inaction, rather than between
various forms of inaction. It would not make much sense to say
that one may not kill oneself by walking into the sea, but may sit
on the beach until submerged by the incoming tide; or that one may
not intentionally lock oneself into a cold storage locker, but may
refrain from coming indoors when the temperature drops below
freezing. Even as a legislative matter, in other words, the intelligent
line does not fall between action and inaction but between those forms
of inaction that consist of abstaining from "ordinary" care and those
that consist of abstaining from "excessive" or "heroic" measures. Unlike action versus inaction, that is not a line to be discerned by logic
or legal analysis, and we should not pretend that it is.

But to return to the principal point for present purposes: the
irrelevance of the action-inaction distinction. Starving oneself to death
is no different from putting a gun to one's temple as far as the common-law definition of suicide is concerned; the cause of death in
both cases is the suicide's conscious decision to "pu[t] an end to his
own existence" (4 *Blackstone*). Of course the common law rejected
the action-inaction distinction in other contexts involving the taking
of human life as well. In the prosecution of a parent for the starvation
death of her infant, it was no defense that the infant's death was
"caused" by no action of the parent but by the natural process of
starvation, or by the infant's natural inability to provide for itself.
A physician, moreover, could be criminally liable for failure to provide care that could have extended the patient's life, even if death
was immediately caused by the underlying disease that the physician
failed to treat.

It is not surprising, therefore, that the early cases considering
the claimed right to refuse medical treatment dismissed as specious
the nice distinction between "passively submitting to death and actively
seeking it. The distinction may be merely verbal, as it would be if

an adult sought death by starvation instead of a drug. If the State may interrupt one mode of self-destruction, it may with equal authority interfere with the other" *John F. Kennedy Memorial Hosp.* v. *Heston* (1971).

The third asserted basis of distinction—that frustrating Nancy Cruzan's wish to die in the present case requires interference with her bodily integrity—is likewise inadequate, because such interference is impermissible only if one begs the question whether her refusal to undergo the treatment on her own is suicide. It has always been lawful not only for the State, but even for private citizens, to interfere with bodily integrity to prevent a felony. . . . It is not even reasonable, much less required by the Constitution, to maintain that although the State has the right to prevent a person from slashing his wrists it does not have the power to apply physical force to prevent him from doing so, nor the power, should he succeed, to apply, coercively if necessary, medical measures to stop the flow of blood. The state-run hospital, I am certain, is not liable under 42 U.S.C. @ 1983 for violation of constitutional rights, nor the private hospital liable under general tort law, if, in a State where suicide is unlawful, it pumps out the stomach of a person who has intentionally taken an overdose of barbiturates, despite that person's wishes to the contrary. . . .

What I have said above is not meant to suggest that I would think it desirable, if we were sure that Nancy Cruzan wanted to die, to keep her alive by the means at issue here. I assert only that the Constitution has nothing to say about the subject. To raise up a constitutional right here we would have to create out of nothing (for it exists neither in text nor tradition) some constitutional principle whereby, although the State may insist that an individual come in out of the cold and eat food, it may not insist that he take medicine; and although it may pump his stomach empty of poison he has ingested, it may not fill his stomach with food he has failed to ingest. Are there, then, no reasonable and humane limits that ought not to be exceeded in requiring an individual to preserve his own life? There obviously are, but they are not set forth in the Due Process Clause. What assures us that those limits will not be exceeded is the same constitutional guarantee that is the source of most of our protection—what protects us, for example, from being assessed a tax of 100 percent of our income above the subsistence level, from being forbidden to drive cars, or from being required to send our children to school for ten hours a day, none of which horribles is categorically prohibited by the Constitution. Our salvation is the Equal Protection Clause, which requires the democratic majority to accept for themselves and their loved ones what they impose on you and me. This Court need not, and has no authority to, inject itself into every field of human activity where irrationality and oppression may theoretically occur, and if it tries to do so it will destroy itself.

DISSENT: JUSTICE BRENNAN, with whom JUSTICE MARSHALL and JUSTICE BLACKMUN join, dissenting.

"Medical technology has effectively created a twilight zone of suspended animation where death commences while life, in some form, continues. Some patients, however, want no part of a life sustained only by medical technology. Instead, they prefer a plan of medical treatment that allows nature to take its course and permits them to die with dignity."

Nancy Cruzan has dwelt in that twilight zone for six years. She is oblivious to her surroundings and will remain so. Her body twitches only reflexively, without consciousness. The areas of her brain that once thought, felt, and experienced sensations have degenerated badly and are continuing to do so. The cavities remaining are filling with cerebrospinal fluid. The "'cerebral cortical atrophy is irreversible, permanent, progressive, and ongoing.'" "Nancy will never interact meaningfully with her environment again. She will remain in a persistent vegetative state until her death."[4] Because she cannot swallow, her nutrition and hydration are delivered through a tube surgically implanted in her stomach.

A grown woman at the time of the accident, Nancy had previously expressed her wish to forgo continuing medical care under circumstances such as these. Her family and her friends are convinced that this is what she would want. A guardian ad litem appointed by the trial court is also convinced that this is what Nancy would want. Yet the Missouri Supreme Court, alone among state courts deciding such a question, has determined that an irreversibly vegetative patient

---

4. Vegetative state patients may react reflexively to sounds, movements and normally painful stimuli, but they do not feel any pain or sense anybody or anything. Vegetative state patients may appear awake but are completely unaware. See Cranford, "The Persistent Vegetative State: The Medical Reality," 18 *Hastings Center Report* 27, 28, 31 (1988).

will remain a passive prisoner of medical technology—for Nancy, perhaps for the next thirty years.

Today the Court, while tentatively accepting that there is some degree of constitutionally protected liberty interest in avoiding unwanted medical treatment, including life-sustaining medical treatment such as artificial nutrition and hydration, affirms the decision of the Missouri Supreme Court. The majority opinion, as I read it, would affirm that decision on the ground that a State may require "clear and convincing" evidence of Nancy Cruzan's prior decision to forgo life-sustaining treatment under circumstances such as hers in order to ensure that her actual wishes are honored. Because I believe that Nancy Cruzan has a fundamental right to be free of unwanted artificial nutrition and hydration, which right is not outweighed by any interests of the State, and because I find that the improperly biased procedural obstacles imposed by the Missouri Supreme Court impermissibly burden that right, I respectfully dissent. Nancy Cruzan is entitled to choose to die with dignity.

"[T]he timing of death—once a matter of fate—is now a matter of human choice." Of the approximately two million people who die each year, 80 percent die in hospitals and long-term care institutions, and perhaps 70 percent of those after a decision to forgo life-sustaining treatment has been made. Nearly every death involves a decision whether to undertake some medical procedure that could prolong the process of dying. Such decisions are difficult and personal. They must be made on the basis of individual values, informed by medical realities, yet within a framework governed by law. The role of the courts is confined to defining that framework, delineating the ways in which government may and may not participate in such decisions.

The question before this Court is a relatively narrow one: whether the Due Process Clause allows Missouri to require a now-incompetent patient in an irreversible persistent vegetative state to remain on life-support absent rigorously clear and convincing evidence that avoiding the treatment represents the patient's prior, express choice. If a fundamental right is at issue, Missouri's rule of decision must be scrutinized under the standards this Court has always applied in such circumstances. As we said in *Zablocki* v. *Redhail* (1978), if a requirement imposed by a State "significantly interferes with the exercise of a fundamental right, it cannot be upheld unless it is supported by sufficiently important state interests and is closely tailored to effectuate only those interests." The Constitution imposes on this Court the obligation to "examine carefully . . . the extent to which [the legitimate government interests advanced] are served by the challenged regulation" *Moore* v. *East Cleveland* (1977). An evidentiary rule, just as a substantive prohibition, must meet these standards if it significantly burdens a fundamental liberty interest. Fundamental rights "are protected not only against heavy-handed frontal attack, but also from being stifled by more subtle governmental interference" *Bates* v. *Little Rock* (1960).

The starting point for our legal analysis must be whether a competent person has a constitutional right to avoid unwanted medical care. Earlier this Term, this Court held that the Due Process Clause of the Fourteenth Amendment confers a significant liberty interest in avoiding unwanted medical treatment. Today, the Court concedes that our prior decisions "support the recognition of a general liberty interest in refusing medical treatment." The Court, however, avoids discussing either the measure of that liberty interest or its application by assuming, for purposes of this case only, that a competent person has a constitutionally protected liberty interest in being free of unwanted artificial nutrition and hydration. Justice O'Connor's opinion is less parsimonious. She openly affirms that "the Court has often deemed state incursions into the body repugnant to the interests protected by the Due Process Clause," that there is a liberty interest in avoiding unwanted medical treatment and that it encompasses the right to be free of "artificially delivered food and water."

But if a competent person has a liberty interest to be free of unwanted medical treatment, as both the majority and Justice O'Connor concede, it must be fundamental. "We are dealing here with [a decision] which involves one of the basic civil rights of men" *Skinner* v. *Oklahoma ex rel. Williamson* (1942). . . .

The right to be free from medical attention without consent, to determine what shall be done with one's own body, is deeply rooted in this nation's traditions, as the majority acknowledges. This right has long been "firmly entrenched in American tort law" and is securely grounded in the earliest common law ("the right to refuse any medical treatment emerged from the doctrines of trespass and battery, which were applied to unauthorized touchings by a physician"). "'Anglo-American law starts with the premise of thorough-going self-determination. It follows that each man is considered to be master of his own body, and he may, if he be of sound mind, expressly prohibit

the performance of lifesaving surgery, or other medical treatment' "
Natanson v. *Kline* (1960). "The inviolability of the person" has been
held as "sacred" and "carefully guarded" as any common law right
(*Union Pacific R. Co.* v. *Botsford* [1891]). Thus, freedom from unwanted medical attention is unquestionably among those principles
"so rooted in the traditions and conscience of our people as to be
ranked as fundamental" *Snyder* v. *Massachusetts* (1934).

That there may be serious consequences involved in refusal of
the medical treatment at issue here does not vitiate the right under
our common-law tradition of medical self-determination. It is "a well-
established rule of general law . . . that it is the patient, not the physician, who ultimately decides if treatment—any treatment—is to be
given at all. . . . The rule has never been qualified in its application by either the nature or purpose of the treatment, or the gravity
of the consequences of acceding to or foregoing it" *Tune* v. *Walter
Reed Army Medical Hosptial* (DC 1985).

No material distinction can be drawn between the treatment to
which Nancy Cruzan continues to be subject—artificial nutrition and
hydration—and any other medical treatment. The artificial delivery
of nutrition and hydration is undoubtedly medical treatment. The
technique to which Nancy Cruzan is subject—artificial feeding through
a gastrostomy tube—involves a tube implanted surgically into her
stomach through incisions in her abdominal wall. . . .

Artificial delivery of food and water is regarded as medical treatment by the medical profession and the Federal Government. According to the American Academy of Neurology, "[t]he artificial provision
of nutrition and hydration is a form of medical treatment . . . analo-
gous to other forms of life-sustaining treatment, such as the use of
the respirator. When a patient is unconscious, both a respirator and
an artificial feeding device serve to support or replace normal bodily
functions that are compromised as a result of the patient's illness.". . . .

Nor does the fact that Nancy Cruzan is now incompetent deprive her of her fundamental rights. . . . As the majority recognizes,
the question is not whether an incompetent has constitutional rights,
but how such rights may be exercised. As we explained in *Thomp-
son* v. *Oklahoma* (1988), "[t]he law must often adjust the manner
in which it affords rights to those whose status renders them unable
to exercise choice freely and rationally. Children, the insane, and those
who are irreversibly ill with loss of brain function, for instance, all

retain 'rights,' to be sure, but often such rights are only meaningful as they are exercised by agents acting with the best interests of their principals in mind." "To deny [its] exercise because the patient is unconscious or incompetent would be to deny the right" *Foody* v. *Manchester Memorial Hospital* (1984).

The right to be free from unwanted medical attention is a right to evaluate the potential benefit of treatment and its possible consequences according to one's own values and to make a personal decision whether to subject oneself to the intrusion. For a patient like Nancy Cruzan, the sole benefit of medical treatment is being kept metabolically alive. Neither artificial nutrition nor any other form of medical treatment available today can cure or in any way ameliorate her condition. Irreversibly vegetative patients are devoid of thought, emotion, and sensation; they are permanently and completely unconscious. As the President's Commission concluded in approving the withdrawal of life support equipment from irreversibly vegetative patients:

"[T]reatment ordinarily aims to benefit a patient through preserving life, relieving pain and suffering, protecting against disability, and returning maximally effective functioning. If a prognosis of permanent unconsciousnes is correct, however, continued treatment cannot confer such benefits. Pain and suffering are absent, as are joy, satisfaction, and pleasure. Disability is total and no return to an even minimal level of social or human functioning is possible."

There are also affirmative reasons why someone like Nancy might choose to forego artificial nutrition and hydration under these circumstances. Dying is personal. And it is profound. For many, the thought of an ignoble end, steeped in decay, is abhorrent. A quiet, proud death, bodily integrity intact, is a matter of extreme consequence. "In certain, thankfully rare, circumstances the burden of maintaining the corporeal existence degrades the very humanity it was meant to serve" *Brophy* v. *New England Sinai Hospital, Inc.* (1986).

Such conditions are, for many, humiliating to contemplate, as is visiting a prolonged and anguished vigil on one's parents, spouse, and children. A long, drawn-out death can have a debilitating effect on family members. For some, the idea of being remembered in their persistent vegetative states rather than as they were before their illness or accident may be very disturbing.[5]

---

5. What general information exists about what most people would choose or would prefer to have chosen for them under these circumstances also indicates the importance of ensuring

Although the right to be free of unwanted medical intervention, like other constitutionally protected interests, may not be absolute, no State interest could outweigh the rights of an individual in Nancy Cruzan's position. Whatever a State's possible interests in mandating life-support treatment under other circumstances, there is no good to be obtained here by Missouri's insistence that Nancy Cruzan remain on life-support systems if it is indeed her wish not to do so. Missouri does not claim, nor could it, that society as a whole will be benefited by Nancy's receiving medical treatment. No third party's situation will be improved and no harm to others will be averted.[6]

The only state interest asserted here is a general interest in the preservation of life. But the State has no legitimate general interest in someone's life, completely abstracted from the interest of the person living that life, that could outweigh the person's choice to avoid medical treatment. "[T]he regulation of constitutionally protected decisions . . . must be predicated on legitimate state concerns other than disagreement with the choice the individual has made. . . . Otherwise, the interest in liberty protected by the Due Process Clause would be a nullity" *Hodgson* v. *Minnesota* (1990). Thus, the State's general interest in life must accede to Nancy Cruzan's particularized

---

a means for now-incompetent patients to exercise their right to avoid unwanted medical treatment. A 1988 poll conducted by the American Medical Association found that 80 percent of those surveyed favored withdrawal of life support systems from hopelessly ill or irreversibly comatose patients if they or their families requested it. (*New York Times,* June 5, 1988, p. 14, col. 4 [citing *American Medical News,* June 3, 1988, p. 9, col. 1]). Another 1988 poll conducted by the Colorado University Graduate School of Public Affairs showed that 85 percent of those questioned would not want to have their own lives maintained with artificial nutrition and hydration if they became permanently unconscious.

6. Were such interests at stake, however, I would find that the Due Process Clause places limits on what invasive medical procedures could be forced on an unwilling comatose patient in pursuit of the interests of a third party. If Missouri were correct that its interests outweigh Nancy's interest in avoiding medical procedures as long as she is free of pain and physical discomfort, it is not apparent why a State could not choose to remove one of her kidneys without consent on the ground that society would be better off if the recipient of that kidney were saved from renal poisoning. Nancy cannot feel surgical pain. Nor would removal of one kidney be expected to shorten her life expectancy. Patches of her skin could also be removed to provide grafts for burn victims, and scrapings of bone marrow to provide grafts for someone with leukemia. Perhaps the State could lawfully remove more vital organs for transplanting into others who would then be cured of their ailments, provided the State placed Nancy on some other life-support equipment to replace the lost function. Indeed, why could the State not perform medical experiments on her body, experiments that might save countless lives, and would cause her no greater burden than she already bears by being fed through the gastrostomy tube? This would be too brave a new world for me and, I submit, for our Constitution.

and intense interest in self-determination in her choice of medical treatment. There is simply nothing legitimately within the State's purview to be gained by superseding her decision.

Moreover, there may be considerable danger that Missouri's rule of decision would impair rather than serve any interest the State does have in sustaining life. Current medical practice recommends use of heroic measures if there is a scintilla of a chance that the patient will recover, on the assumption that the measures will be discontinued should the patient improve. When the President's Commission in 1982 approved the withdrawal of life support equipment from irreversibly vegetative patients, it explained that "[a]n even more troubling wrong occurs when a treatment that might save life or improve health is not started because the health care personnel are afraid that they will find it very difficult to stop the treatment if, as is fairly likely, it proves to be of little benefit and greatly burdens the patient." A New Jersey court recognized that families as well as doctors might be discouraged by an inability to stop life-support measures from "even attempting certain types of care [which] could thereby force them into hasty and premature decisions to allow a patient to die" *In re Conroy* (1985).

This is not to say that the State has no legitimate interests to assert here. As the majority recognizes, Missouri has a parens patriae interest in providing Nancy Cruzan, now incompetent, with as accurate as possible a determination of how she would exercise her rights under these circumstances. Second, if and when it is determined that Nancy Cruzan would want to continue treatment, the State may legitimately assert an interest in providing that treatment. But until Nancy's wishes have been determined, the only state interest that may be asserted is an interest in safeguarding the accuracy of that determination.

Accuracy, therefore, must be our touchstone. Missouri may constitutionally impose only those procedural requirements that serve to enhance the accuracy of a determination of Nancy Cruzan's wishes or are at least consistent with an accurate determination. The Missouri "safeguard" that the Court upholds today does not meet that standard. The determination needed in this context is whether the incompetent person would choose to live in a persistent vegetative state on life support or to avoid this medical treatment. Missouri's rule of decision imposes a markedly asymmetrical evidentiary burden. Only evidence of specific statements of treatment choice made by the patient when competent is admissible to support a finding that the patient, now in a persistent vegetative state, would wish to avoid further medical treatment. Moreover, this evidence must be clear and convincing. No proof is required to support a finding that the incompetent person would wish to continue treatment.

The majority offers several justifications for Missouri's heightened evidentiary standard. First, the majority explains that the State may constitutionally adopt this rule to govern determinations of an incompetent's wishes in order to advance the State's substantive interests, including its unqualified interest in the preservation of human life. Missouri's evidentiary standard, however, cannot rest on the State's own interest in a particular substantive result. To be sure, courts have long erected clear and convincing evidence standards to place the greater risk of erroneous decisions on those bringing disfavored claims. In such cases, however, the choice to discourage certain claims was a legitimate, constitutional policy choice. In contrast, Missouri has no such power to disfavor a choice by Nancy Cruzan to avoid medical treatment, because Missouri has no legitimate interest in providing Nancy with treatment until it is established that this represents her choice. Just as a State may not override Nancy's choice directly, it may not do so indirectly through the imposition of a procedural rule.

Second, the majority offers two explanations for why Missouri's clear and convincing evidence standard is a means of enhancing accuracy, but neither is persuasive. The majority initially argues that a clear and convincing evidence standard is necessary to compensate for the possibility that such proceedings will lack the "guarantee of accurate factfinding that the adversary process brings with it," citing *Ohio* v. *Akron Center for Reproductive Health* (1990). Without supporting the Court's decision in that case, I note that the proceeding to determine an incompetent's wishes is quite different from a proceeding to determine whether a minor may bypass notifying her parents before undergoing an abortion on the ground that she is mature enough to make the decision or that the abortion is in her best interests.

An adversarial proceeding is of particular importance when one side has a strong personal interest which needs to be counterbalanced to assure the court that the question will be fully explored. A minor who has a strong interest in obtaining permission for an abortion without notifying her parents may come forward whether or not society would be satisfied that she has made the decision with the seasoned judgment of an adult. The proceeding here is of a different nature. Barring venal motives, which a trial court has the means of ferreting out, the decision to come forward to request a judicial order to stop treatment represents a slowly and carefully considered resolution by at least one adult and more frequently several adults that discontinuation of treatment is the patient's wish.

In addition, the bypass procedure at issue in *Akron* is ex parte and secret. The court may not notify the minor's parents, siblings, or friends. No one may be present to submit evidence unless brought forward by the minor herself. In contrast, the proceeding to determine Nancy Cruzan's wishes was neither ex parte nor secret. In a hearing to determine the treatment preferences of an incompetent person, a court is not limited to adjusting burdens of proof as its only means of protecting against a possible imbalance. Indeed, any concern that those who come forward will present a one-sided view would be better addressed by appointing a guardian ad litem, who could use the State's powers of discovery to gather and present evidence regarding the patient's wishes. A guardian ad litem's task is to uncover any conflicts of interest and ensure that each party likely to have relevant evidence is consulted and brought forward—for example, other members of the family, friends, clergy, and doctors. Missouri's heightened evidentiary standard attempts to achieve balance by discounting evidence; the guardian ad litem technique achieves balance by probing for additional evidence. Where, as here, the family members, friends, doctors, and guardian ad litem agree, it is not because the process has failed, as the majority suggests. It is because there is no genuine dispute as to Nancy's preference.

The majority next argues that where, as here, important individual rights are at stake, a clear and convincing evidence standard has long been held to be an appropriate means of enhancing accuracy, citing decisions concerning what process an individual is due before he can be deprived of a liberty interest.

The majority claims that the allocation of the risk of error is justified because it is more important not to terminate life-support for someone who would wish it continued than to honor the wishes of someone who would not. An erroneous decision to terminate life-support is irrevocable, says the majority, while an erroneous decision not to terminate "results in a maintenance of the status quo." But, from the point of view of the patient, an erroneous decision in either direction is irrevocable. An erroneous decision to terminate artificial nutrition and hydration, to be sure, will lead to failure of that last remnant of physiological life, the brain stem, and result in complete brain death. An erroneous decision not to terminate life-support, however, robs a patient of the very qualities protected by the right to avoid unwanted medical treatment. His own degraded existence is perpetuated; his family's suffering is protracted; the memory he leaves behind becomes more and more distorted. . . .

Even more than its heightened evidentiary standard, the Missouri court's categorical exclusion of relevant evidence dispenses with any semblance of accurate factfinding. The court adverted to no evidence supporting its decision, but held that no clear and convincing, inherently reliable evidence had been presented to show that Nancy would want to avoid further treatment. In doing so, the court failed to consider statements Nancy had made to family members and a close friend.[7] The court also failed to consider testimony from Nancy's

---

7. The trial court had relied on the testimony of Athena Comer, a long-time friend, co-worker, and a housemate for several months, as sufficient to show that Nancy Cruzan would wish to be free of medical treatment under her present circumstances. Ms. Comer described a conversation she and Nancy had while living together, concerning Ms. Comer's sister who had become ill suddenly and died during the night. The Comer family had been told that if she had lived through the night, she would have been in a vegetative state. Nancy had lost a grandmother a few months before. Ms. Comer testified that: "Nancy said that she would never want to live [as a vegetative state] because if she couldn't be normal or even, you know, like half way, and do things for yourself, because Nancy always did, that she didn't want to live . . . and we talked about it a lot." She said "several times" that "she wouldn't want to live that way because if she was going to live, she wanted to be able to live, not to just lay in a bed and not be able to move because you can't do anything for yourself." "[S]he said that she hoped that [all the] people in her family knew that she wouldn't want to live [as a vegetable] because she knew it was usually up to the family whether you lived that way or not."

The conversation took place approximately a year before Nancy's accident and was described by Ms. Comer as a "very serious" conversation that continued for approximately half an hour without interruption. The Missouri Supreme Court dismissed Nancy's statement as "unreliable" on the ground that it was an informally expressed reaction to other people's medical conditions.

The Missouri Supreme Court did not refer to other evidence of Nancy's wishes or explain why it was rejected. Nancy's sister Christy, to whom she was very close, testified that she and Nancy had had two very serious conversations about a year and a half before the accident. A day or two after their niece was stillborn (but would have been badly damaged if she had lived), Nancy had said that maybe it was part of a "greater plan" that the baby had been stillborn and did not have to face "the possible life of mere existence." A month later, after their grandmother had died after a long battle with heart problems, Nancy said that "it was better for my grandmother not to be kind of brought back and forth [by] medical [treatment], brought back from a critical near point of death. . . . "

mother and sister that they were certain that Nancy would want to discontinue artificial nutrition and hydration,[8] even after the court found that Nancy's family was loving and without malignant motive. The court also failed to consider the conclusions of the guardian ad litem, appointed by the trial court, that there was clear and convincing evidence that Nancy would want to discontinue medical treatment and that this was in her best interests. The court did not specifically define what kind of evidence it would consider clear and convincing, but its general discussion suggests that only a living will or equivalently formal directive from the patient when competent would meet this standard.

Too few people execute living wills or equivalently formal directives for such an evidentiary rule to ensure adequately that the wishes of incompetent persons will be honored. While it might be a wise social policy to encourage people to furnish such instructions, no general conclusion about a patient's choice can be drawn from the absence of formalities. The probability of becoming irreversibly vegetative is so low that many people may not feel an urgency to marshal formal evidence of their preferences. Some may not wish to dwell on their own physical deterioration and mortality. Even someone with a resolute determination to avoid life-support under circumstances such as Nancy's would still need to know that such things as living wills exist and how to execute one. Often legal help would be necessary, especially given the majority's apparent willingness to permit States to insist that a person's wishes are not truly known unless the particular medical treatment is specified.

As a California appellate court observed: "The lack of generalized public awareness of the statutory scheme and the typically human characteristics of procrastination and reluctance to contemplate the need for such arrangements, however, makes this a tool which will all too often go unused by those who might desire it." When a person tells family or close friends that she does not want her life sustained artificially, she is "express[ing] her wishes in the only terms familiar

---

8. Nancy's sister Christy, Nancy's mother, and another of Nancy's friends testified that Nancy would want to discontinue the hydration and nutrition. Christy said that "Nancy would be horrified at the state she is in." She would also "want to take that burden away from [her family]." Based on "a lifetime of experience [I know Nancy's wishes] are to discontinue the hydration and the nutrition." Nancy's mother testified: "Nancy would not want to be like she is now. [I]f it were me up there or Christy or any of us, she would be doing for us what we are trying to do for her. I know she would, . . . as her mother."

to her, and . . . as clearly as a lay person should be asked to express them. To require more is unrealistic, and for all practical purposes, it precludes the rights of patients to forgo life-sustaining treatment" *In re O'Connor* (1988). When Missouri enacted a living will statute, it specifically provided that the absence of a living will does not warrant a presumption that a patient wishes continued medical treatment. Thus, apparently not even Missouri's own legislature believes that a person who does not execute a living will fails to do so because he wishes continuous medical treatment under all circumstances.

The testimony of close friends and family members, on the other hand, may often be the best evidence available of what the patient's choice would be. It is they with whom the patient most likely will have discussed such questions and they who know the patient best. "Family members have a unqiue knowledge of the patient which is vital to any decision on his or her behalf."

The Missouri court's disdain for Nancy's statements in serious conversations not long before her accident, for the opinions of Nancy's family and friends as to her values, beliefs, and certain choice, and even for the opinion of an outside objective factfinder appointed by the State evinces a disdain for Nancy Cruzan's own right to choose. The rules by which an incompetent person's wishes are determined must represent every effort to determine those wishes. The rule that the Missouri court adopted and that this Court upholds, however, skews the result away from a determination that as accurately as possible reflects the individual's own preferences and beliefs. It is a rule that transforms human beings into passive subjects of medical technology.

"[M]edical care decisions must be guided by the individual patient's interests and values. Allowing persons to determine their own medical treatment is an important way in which society respects persons as individuals. Moreover, the respect due to persons as individuals does not diminish simply because they have become incapable of participating in treatment decisions. . . . [I]t is still possible for others to make a decision that reflects [the patient's] interests more closely than would a purely technological decision to do whatever is possible. Lacking the ability to decide, [a patient] has a right to a decision that takes his interests into account" *In re Drabick* (1988).

I do not suggest that States must sit by helplessly if the choices of incompetent patients are in danger of being ignored. Even if the

Court had ruled that Missouri's rule of decision is unconstitutional, as I believe it should have, States would nevertheless remain free to fashion procedural protections to safeguard the interests of incompetents under these circumstances. The Constitution provides merely a framework here: protections must be genuinely aimed at ensuring decisions commensurate with the will of the patient, and must be reliable as instruments to that end. Of the many States which have instituted such protections, Missouri is virtually the only one to have fashioned a rule that lessens the likelihood of accurate determinations. In contrast, nothing in the Constitution prevents States from reviewing the advisability of a family decision, by requiring a court proceeding or by appointing an impartial guardian ad litem.

There are various approaches to determining an incompetent patient's treatment choice in use by the several States today and there may be advantages and disadvantages to each and other approaches not yet envisioned. The choice, in largest part, is and should be left to the States, so long as each State is seeking, in a reliable manner, to discover what the patient would want. But with such momentous interests in the balance, States must avoid procedures that will prejudice the decision. "To err either way—to keep a person alive under circumstances under which he would rather have been allowed to die, or to allow that person to die when he would have chosen to cling to life—would be deeply unfortunate" *In re Conroy.*

Finally, I cannot agree with the majority that where it is not possible to determine what choice an incompetent patient would make, a State's role as parens patriae permits the State automatically to make that choice itself. . . .

The majority justifies its position by arguing that, while close family members may have a strong feeling about the question, "there is no automatic assurance that the view of close family members will necessarily be the same as the patient's would have been had she been confronted with the prospect of her situation while competent." I cannot quarrel with this observation. But it leads only to another question: Is there any reason to suppose that a State is more likely to make the choice that the patient would have made than someone who knew the patient intimately? To ask this is to answer it. As the New Jersey Supreme Court observed: "Family members are best qualified to make substituted judgments for incompetent patients not only because of their peculiar grasp of the patient's approach to life, but also because of their special bonds with him or her. . . . It is . . . they who treat the patient as a person, rather than a symbol of a cause" *In re Jobes* (1987). The State, in contrast, is a stranger to the patient.

A State's inability to discern an incompetent patient's choice still need not mean that a State is rendered powerless to protect that choice. But I would find that the Due Process Clause prohibits a State from doing more than that. A State may ensure that the person who makes the decision on the patient's behalf is the one whom the patient himself would have selected to make that choice for him. And a State may exclude from consideration anyone having improper motives. But a State generally would either repose the choice with the person whom the patient himself would most likely have chosen as proxy or leave the decision to the patient's family.[9]

. . . Yet Missouri and this Court have displaced Nancy's own assessment of the processes associated with dying. They have discarded evidence of her will, ignored her values, and deprived her of the right to a decision as closely approximating her own choice as humanly possible. They have done so disingenuously in her name, and openly in Missouri's own. That Missouri and this Court may truly be motivated only by concern for incompetent patients makes no matter. As one of our most prominent jurists warned us decades ago: "Experience should teach us to be most on our guard to protect liberty when the government's purposes are beneficent. . . . The greatest dangers to liberty lurk in insidious encroachment by men of zeal, well meaning but without understanding" *Olmstead* v. *United States* (1928).

I respectfully dissent.

JUSTICE STEVENS, dissenting.

Our Constitution is born of the proposition that all legitimate governments must secure the equal right of every person to "Life, Liberty, and the pursuit of Happiness." In the ordinary case we quite naturally assume that these three ends are compatible, mutually enhancing, and perhaps even coincident.

The Court would make an exception here. It permits the State's

---

9. Only in the exceedingly rare case where the State cannot find any family member or friend who can be trusted to endeavor genuinely to make the treatment choice the patient would have made does the State become the legitimate surrogate decisionmaker.

abstract, undifferentiated interest in the preservation of life to over-whelm the best interests of Nancy Beth Cruzan, interests which would, according to an undisputed finding, be served by allowing her guard-ians to exercise her constitutional right to discontinue medical treat-ment. Ironically, the Court reaches this conclusion despite endorsing three significant propositions which should save it from any such dilemma. First, a competent individual's decision to refuse life-sus-taining medical procedures is an aspect of liberty protected by the Due Process Clause of the Fourteenth Amendment. Second, upon a proper evidentiary showing, a qualified guardian may make that decision on behalf of an incompetent ward. Third, in answering the important question presented by this tragic case, it is wise "not to attempt by any general statement, to cover every possible phase of the subject." Together, these considerations suggest that Nancy Cru-zan's liberty to be free from medical treatment must be understood in light of the facts and circumstances particular to her.

I would so hold: in my view, the Constitution requires the State to care for Nancy Cruzan's life in a way that gives appropriate re-spect to her own best interests. . . .

[According to the trial judge,] "There is a fundamental natural right expressed in our Consittution as the 'right to liberty,' which permits an individual to refuse or direct the withholding or withdrawal of artificial death-prolonging procedures when the person has no more cognitive brain function than our ward and all the physicians agree there is no hope of further recovery while deterioration of the brain continues with further overall worsening physical contractures. To the extent of nutrition and hydration or euthanasia or mercy killing, if such be the definition, under all circumstances, arbitrarily and with no exceptions, it is in violation of our ward's constitutional rights by depriving her of liberty without due process of law. To decide otherwise that medical treatment once undertaken must be continued irrespective of its lack of success or benefit to the patient in effect gives one's body to medical science without their consent. . . ."

Because he believed he had a duty to do so, the independent guard-ian ad litem appealed the trial court's order to the Missouri Supreme Court. In that appeal, however, the guardian advised the court that he did not disagree with the trial court's decision. Specifically, he endorsed the critical finding that "it was in Nancy Cruzan's best in-terests to have the tube feeding discontinued."

That important conclusion thus was not disputed by the litigants. One might reasonably suppose that it would be dispositive: if Nancy Cruzan has no interest in continued treatment, and if she has a liberty interest in being free from unwanted treatment, and if the cessation of treatment would have no adverse impact on third parties, and if no reason exists to doubt the good faith of Nancy's parents, then what possible basis could the State have for insisting upon continued medical treatment? Yet, instead of questioning or endorsing the trial court's conclusions about Nancy Cruzan's interests, the State Supreme Court largely ignored them. . . .

The portion of this Court's opinion that considers the merits of this case is similarly unsatisfactory. It, too, fails to respect the best interests of the patient. It, too, relies on what is tantamount to a waiver rationale: the dying patient's best interests are put to one side and the entire inquiry is focused on her prior expressions of intent. An innocent person's constitutional right to be free from unwanted medical treatment is thereby categorically limited to those patients who had the foresight to make an unambiguous statement of their wishes while competent. The Court's decision affords no protection to children, to young people who are victims of unexpected accidents or illnesses, or to the countless thousands of elderly persons who either fail to decide, or fail to explain, how they want to be treated if they should experience a similar fate. Because Nancy Beth Cruzan did not have the foresight to preserve her constitutional right in a living will, or some comparable "clear and convincing" alternative, her right is gone forever and her fate is in the hands of the state legislature instead of in those of her family, her independent neutral guardian ad litem, and an impartial judge—all of whom agree on the course of action that is in her best interests. The Court's willingness to find a waiver of this constitutional right reveals a distressing misunderstanding of the importance of individual liberty. . . .

Nancy Cruzan's interest in life, no less than that of any other person, includes an interest in how she will be thought of after her death by those whose opinions mattered to her. There can be no doubt that her life made her dear to her family, and to others. How she dies will affect how that life is remembered. The trial court's order authorizing Nancy's parents to cease their daughter's treatment would have permitted the family that cares for Nancy to bring to a close her tragedy and her death. Missouri's objection to that order subordinates Nancy's body, her family, and the lasting significance of her life to the State's own interests. The decision we review thereby interferes with constitutional interests of the highest order.

Missouri asserts that its policy is related to a state interest in the protection of life. In my view, however, it is an effort to define life, rather than to protect it, that is the heart of Missouri's policy. Missouri insists, without regard to Nancy Cruzan's own interests, upon equating her life with the biological persistence of her bodily functions. Nancy Cruzan, it must be remembered, is not now simply incompetent. She is in a persistent vegetative state, and has been so for seven years. The trial court found, and no party contested, that Nancy has no possibility of recovery and no consciousness.

It seems to me that the Court errs insofar as it characterizes this case as involving "judgments about the 'quality' of life that a particular individual may enjoy." Nancy Cruzan is obviously "alive" in a physiological sense. But for patients like Nancy Cruzan, who have no consciousness and no chance of recovery, there is a serious question as to whether the mere persistence of their bodies is "life" as that word is commonly understood, or as it is used in both the Constitution and the Declaration of Independence. The State's unflagging determination to perpetuate Nancy Cruzan's physical existence is comprehensible only as an effort to define life's meaning, not as an attempt to preserve its sanctity.

This much should be clear from the oddity of Missouri's definition alone. Life, particularly human life, is not commonly thought of as a merely physiological condition or function. Its sanctity is often thought to derive from the impossibility of any such reduction. When people speak of life, they often mean to describe the experiences that comprise a person's history, as when it is said that somebody "led a good life." They may also mean to refer to the practical manifestation of the human spirit, a meaning captured by the familiar observation that somebody "added life" to an assembly. If there is a shared thread among the various opinions on this subject, it may be that life is an activity which is at once the matrix for and an integration of a person's interests. In any event, absent some theological abstraction, the idea of life is not conceived separately from the idea of a living person. Yet, it is by precisely such a separation that Missouri asserts an interest in Nancy Cruzan's life in opposition to Nancy Cruzan's own interests. The resulting definition is uncommon indeed. . . .

In short, there is no reasonable ground for believing that Nancy Beth Cruzan has any personal interest in the perpetuation of what the State has decided in her life. As I have already suggested, it would be possible to hypothesize such an interest on the basis of theological or philosophical conjecture. But even to posit such a basis for the State's action is to condemn it. It is not within the province of secular government to circumscribe the liberties of the people by regulations designed wholly for the purpose of establishing a sectarian definition of life.

My disagreement with the Court is thus unrelated to its endorsement of the clear and convincing standard of proof for cases of this kind. Indeed, I agree that the controlling facts must be established with unmistakable clarity. The critical question, however, is not how to prove the controlling facts but rather what proven facts should be controlling. In my view, the constitutional answer is clear: the best interests of the individual, especially when buttressed by the interests of all related third parties, must prevail over any general state policy that simply ignores those interests. Indeed, the only apparent secular basis for the State's interest in life is the policy's persuasive impact upon people other than Nancy and her family. Yet, "[a]lthough the State may properly perform a teaching function," and although that teaching may foster respect for the sanctity of life, the State may not pursue its project by infringing constitutionally protected interests for "symbolic effect" *Carey* v. *Population Services International* (1977). . . .

Only because Missouri has abrogated to itself the power to define life, and only because the Court permits this usurpation, are Nancy Cruzan's life and liberty put into disquieting conflict. If Nancy Cruzan's life were defined by reference to her own interests, so that her life expired when her biological existence ceased serving any of her own interests, then her constitutionally protected interest in freedom from unwanted treatment would not come into conflict with her constitutionally protected interest in life. Conversely, if there were any evidence that Nancy Cruzan herself defined life to encompass every form of biological persistence by a human being, so that the continuation of treatment would serve Nancy's own liberty, then once again there would be no conflict between life and liberty. The opposition of life and liberty in this case is thus not the result of Nancy Cruzan's tragic accident, but is instead the artificial consequence of Missouri's effort, and this Court's willingness, to abstract Nancy Cruzan's life from Nancy Cruzan's person. . . .

There is, however, nothing "hypothetical" about Nancy Cruzan's constitutionally protected interest in freedom from unwanted treatment, and the difficulties involved in ascertaining what her interests are do not in any way justify the State's decision to oppose her interests with its own. As this case comes to us, the crucial question—and the question addressed by the Court—is not what Nancy Cruzan's interests are, but whether the State must give effect to them. There is certainly nothing novel about the practice of permitting a next friend to assert constitutional rights on behalf of an incompetent patient who is unable to do so. Thus, if Nancy Cruzan's incapacity to "exercise" her rights is to alter the balance between her interests and the State's, there must be some further explanation of how it does so. The Court offers two possibilities, neither of them satisfactory.

The first possibility is that the State's policy favoring life is by its nature less intrusive upon the patient's interest than any alternative. The Court suggests that Missouri's policy "results in a maintenance of the status quo," and is subject to reversal, while a decision to terminate treatment "is not susceptible of correction" because death is irreversible. Yet, this explanation begs the question, for it assumes either that the State's policy is consistent with Nancy Cruzan's own interests, or that no damage is done by ignoring her interests. The first assumption is without basis in the record of this case, and would obviate any need for the State to rely, as it does, upon its own interests rather than upon the patient's. The second assumption is unconscionable. Insofar as Nancy Cruzan has an interest in being remembered for how she lived rather than how she died, the damage done to those memories by the prolongation of her death is irreversible. Insofar as Nancy Cruzan has an interest in the cessation of any pain, the continuation of her pain is irreversible. Insofar as Nancy Cruzan has an interest in a closure to her life consistent with her own beliefs rather than those of the Missouri legislature, the state's imposition of its contrary view is irreversible. To deny the importance of these consequences is in effect to deny that Nancy Cruzan has interests at all, and thereby to deny her personhood in the name of preserving the sanctity of her life.

The second possibility is that the State must be allowed to define the interests of incompetent patients with respect to life-sustaining treatment because there is no procedure capable of determining what those interests are in any particular case. The Court points out various possible "abuses" and inaccuracies that may affect procedures authorizing the termination of treatment. The Court correctly notes that in some cases there may be a conflict between the interests of an incompetent patient and the interests of members of her family. A State's procedures must guard against the risk that the survivors' interests are not mistaken for the patient's. Yet, the appointment of the natural guardian ad litem, coupled with the searching inquiry conducted by the trial judge and the imposition of the clear and convincing standard of proof, all effectively avoided that risk in this case. Why such procedural safeguards should not be adequate to avoid a similar risk in other cases is a question the Court simply ignores.

Indeed, to argue that the mere possibility of error in any case suffices to allow the State's interests to override the particular interests of incompetent individuals in every case, or to argue that the interests of such individuals are unknowable and therefore must be subordinated to the State's concerns, is once again to deny Nancy Cruzan's personhood. The meaning of respect for her personhood, and for that of others who are gravely ill and incapacitated, is, admittedly, not easily defined: choices about life and death are profound ones, not susceptible of resolution by recourse to medical or legal rules. It may be that the best we can do is to ensure that these choices are made by those who will care enough about the patient to investigate her interests with particularity and caution. The Court seems to recognize as much when it cautions against formulating any general or inflexible rule to govern all the cases that might arise in this area of the law. The Court's deference to the legislature is, however, itself an inflexible rule, one that the Court is willing to apply in this case even though the Court's principal grounds for deferring to Missouri's legislature are hypothetical circumstances not relevant to Nancy Cruzan's interests.

On either explanation, then, the Court's deference seems ultimately to derive from the premise that chronically incompetent persons have no constitutionally cognizable interests at all, and so are not persons within the meaning of the Constitution. Deference of this sort is patently unconstitutional. It is also dangerous in ways that may not be immediately apparent. Today the State of Missouri has announced its intent to spend several hundred thousand dollars in preserving the life of Nancy Beth Cruzan in order to vindicate its general policy favoring the preservation of human life. Tomorrow, another State equally eager to champion an interest in the "quality of life" might favor a policy designed to ensure quick and comfortable deaths by denying treatment to categories of marginally hopeless cases. If the State in fact has an interest in defining life, and if the State's policy with respect to the termination of life-sustaining treatment commands deference from the judiciary, it is unclear how any resulting conflict between the best interests of the individual and the general policy of the State would be resolved. I believe the Constitution requires that the individual's vital interest in liberty should prevail over the general policy in that case, just as in this.

That a contrary result is readily imaginable under the majority's theory makes manifest that this Court cannot defer to any State policy that drives a theoretical wedge between a person's life, on the one hand, and that person's liberty or happiness, on the other. The consequence of such a theory is to deny the personhood of those whose lives are defined by the State's interests rather than their own. This consequence may be acceptable in theology or in speculative philosophy, but it is radically inconsistent with the foundation of all legitimate government. Our Constitution presupposes a respect for the personhood of every individual, and nowhere is strict adherence to that principle more essential than in the Judicial Branch. . . .

The Cruzan family's continuing concern provides a concrete reminder that Nancy Cruzan's interests did not disappear with her vitality or her consciousness. However commendable may be the State's interest in human life, it cannot pursue that interest by appropriating Nancy Cruzan's life as a symbol for its own purposes. Lives do not exist in abstraction from persons, and to pretend otherwise is not to honor but to desecrate the State's responsibility for protecting life. A State that seeks to demonstrate its commitment to life may do so by aiding those who are actively struggling for life and health. In this endeavor, unfortunately, no State can lack for opportunities: there can be no need to make an example of tragic cases like that of Nancy Cruzan.

I respectfully dissent.

Glossary

Amniocentesis: taking a test sample of the fluid that surrounds the fetus

Apnea: transient cessation of breathing

A priori: logically prior to or independent of sense experience

Benemortasia: good death

Cachectic: state of extreme ill health characterized by malnutrition, anemia, and weakness

Carbon dioxide narcosis: stupor or insensibility produced by excessive carbon dioxide

Cellular-pathogenic process: a process giving origin to disease in the cells

Curare: drug used to paralyze muscles during surgery

Cytotoxic: poisonous to cells

Decubitus: posture of a patient who has been lying in bed for an extended period

Discerebrate condition: disruption of mental functioning

Endorphins: any of a group of proteins occurring in the brain and having analgesic (pain killing) properties

Endotracheal intubation: insertion of a tube down the trachea in giving anesthesia or to help the patient breathe

Fetology: branch of medicine dealing with the fetus *in utero*

Fibrogen: substance that slows blood circulation

Hemoglobin level: measurement of the pigment in the red blood cells that carry oxygen to the tissues

Hypercapnia: excessive carbon dioxide in the blood
Hypoxia: reduction of oxygen supply to tissues

Intercostal: situated between the ribs

Microencephalitic: abnormal smallness of the brain
Myastenia gravis: a muscular disorder involving fatigue and exhaustion of a muscle group, especially the muscles of the eye, face, lips, tongue, throat, and neck
Myelomeningocoele: defect associated with the spinal cord and its membranes

Necrotic bowel: cell death of a portion of the intestines
Neonate: a newborn
Neuroblastoma: tumor of the nervous system affecting mostly infants and children up to ten years of age

Ontological evil: the imperfection and disorder that is part of nature

Parenteral route: giving of drugs by injection or suppositories (as contrasted with drugs given orally)

Refractory to treatment: impossible to treat
Respiratory insufficiency: failure of the respiratory system to supply adequate oxygen

Solipsism: the view that only the self and its ideas exist
Somatic problems: problems related to the body
Stridor: sharp high sound made when air passes an obstruction in the larynx
Suprasternal: situated above the sterum

Tay-Sach disease: a rare, fatal disease occurring in infants and children, especially of Jewish extraction, a disease characterized by blindness and loss of weight
21-Trisomy newborn: also called Downs Syndrome and formerly called Mongolism—a chromosome disorder characterized by moderate to severe mental retardation and certain bodily features such as a flattened skull and flat-bridge nose

Vitalism: the doctrine that the processes of life are due to a principle distinct from the physiochemical laws

Contributors

S. JAMES ADLESTEIN, M.D., Harvard Medical School.

PIETER ADMIRAAL, M.D., Ph.D., anesthesiologist (Delft, The Netherlands).

CHRISTINE K. CASSELL, M.D., Pritzker School of Medicine, Chicago.

EDWIN H. CASSEM, M.D., Massachusetts General Hospital, Boston.

GERALD D. COLEMAN, S.S., Ph.D., professor of moral and pastoral theology, St. Patrick's Seminary, Menlo Park, California.

RONALD E. CRANFORD, M.D., Hennepin County Medical Center, Minneapolis.

H. TRISTRAM ENGLEHARDT, JR., M.D., Ph.D., professor of philosophy, Rice University, and the Center for Ethics, Baylor College of Medicine, Houston.

JAN VAN EYS, M.D., The University of Texas Cancer Center and School of Medicine, Houston.

DANIEL D. FEDERMAN, M.D., Harvard Medical School.

JOSEPH FLETCHER, Visiting Scholar of Medical Ethics at the University of Virginia, and Robert Treat Paine Professor Emeritus at the Episcopal Theological School (Harvard University).

WILLIARD GAYLIN, M.D., president of the Hastings Center, Briarcliff Manor, New York.

J. GAY-WILLIAMS, no biographical information is available—Eds.

EDWARD W. HOOK, M.D., University of Virginia Medical Center, Charlottesville.

LEON R. KASS, M.D., The Committee on Thought, the University of Chicago.

C. EVERETT KOOP, M.D., Sc.D., former Surgeon General of the United States.

GERALD A. LARUE, Ph.D., President Emeritus of the National Hemlock Society, Professor Emeritus of Archaeology and Biblical History and adjunct professor of gerontology (Ethel Percy Andrus Gerontology Center) University of Southern California.

BERNARD LO, M.D., University of California School of Medicine, San Francisco.

CHARLES G. MOERTEL, M.D., Mayo Clinic and Medical School, Rochester, Minnesota.

EDMUND D. PELLEGRINO, M.D., The Kennedy Institute of Ethics, Georgetown University.

JAMES RACHELS, Ph.D., professor of philosophy, the University of Alabama, Birmingham.

PETER SAFAR, M.D., The International Resuscitation Research Center, University of Pittsburgh Medical School.

D. ALAN SHEWMON, M.D., assistant professor of pediatrics, Division of Neurology, University of California, Los Angeles.

MARK SIEGLER, M.D., The Center for Clinical Medical Ethics, the University of Chicago.

ALAN STONE, M.D., Harvard Law School.

THOMAS SULLIVAN, Ph.D., associate professor of philosophy, St. Thomas College, St. Paul, Minnesota.

KENNETH L. VAUX, Ph.D., Department of Ethics in Medicine, the University of Illinois Medical Center, Chicago.

SIDNEY WANZER, M.D., Concord Hillside Medical Center, Concord Massachusetts.

CHRISTINE WICKER, writer for the *Dallas Morning News*.

ERNLÉ W. D. YOUNG, Ph.D., Chaplaincy Service, Stanford University Hospital.